Cattle, Sheep, Goats, and Antelope
(the Bovidae Family)

PAT MORRIS, AMY-JANE BEER

About This Volume

This volume is about the largest of the herbivore families, the Bovidae, which includes cattle, sheep, goats, and antelope. These herbivores, together with the giraffes and deer in the previous volume, are often referred to as ungulates, because they walk on hooves that are derived from the tips of their fingers and toes. These animals are also ruminants – a group of mammals that are very well adapted to live on vegetation.

The cattle family includes some of the most important domestic mammals. Some cattle have been partners with humans for many thousands of years and are now widespread throughout the world. None of the other three groups of ungulates have been so fully domesticated.

Published by Simply Home Entertainment
Bentima House
168–172 Old Street
London EC1V 9BP

The BBC is not responsible for the content of this volume.

For this edition:
Editorial Director:	Lindsey Lowe
Managing Editor:	Deborah Evans
Creative Director:	Jeni Child
Designer:	John Dinsdale
Picture Researcher:	Sophie Mortimer
Production Director:	Alastair Gourlay
Production:	Richard Berry

Printed in China

ISSN 1758-0994

Coming in Volume 12: Burrowers & Builders
Beavers, Squirrels, Chipmunks and other rodents

On your DVD:
Burrowers & Builders;
Overground &
Underground

Contents

When startled, springboks can be seen pronking—jumping in the air with the back arched and legs pointing downwards.

Members of the cattle, sheep, goat, and antelope family are widespread and varied, including the yak (left), the impala (above), the bighorn sheep (below), and the ibex (right).

How to Use This Set

Ultimate Wildlife is a multi-volume set that describes in detail animals from all corners of the earth. Each volume brings together those animals that are most closely related and have similar lifestyles. For more information on how scientists group animals together and name them, see overleaf. In this series, all the meat-eating mammals (carnivores) are in the first couple of volumes, while other volumes look at, for example, sea mammals, such as whales and dolphins, or rodents.

Article Styles

You will find three kinds of article in this series. There are two types of introductory or overview article: one introduces large animal groups or orders (such as the cetaceans) and the other introduces smaller groups or families (such as hyenas). The articles review the full variety of animals to be found in different groups.

However, the majority of the articles making up each volume concentrates on describing individual animals in great detail. Each article starts with a fact-filled data panel to help you gather information at-a-glance. Used together the different styles of article enable you to become

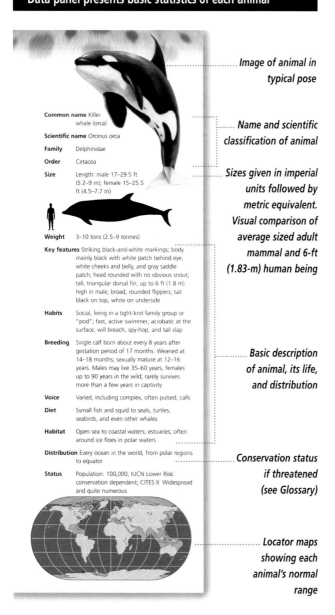

Data panel presents basic statistics of each animal

Image of animal in typical pose

Common name Killer whale (orca)

Scientific name *Orcinus orca*

Family Delphinidae

Order Cetacea

Size Length: male 17–29.5 ft (5.2–9 m); female 15–25.5 ft (4.5–7.7 m)

Name and scientific classification of animal

Sizes given in imperial units followed by metric equivalent. Visual comparison of average sized adult mammal and 6-ft (1.83-m) human being

Weight 3–10 tons (2.5–9 tonnes)

Key features Striking black-and-white markings; body mainly black with white patch behind eye, white cheeks and belly, and gray saddle patch; head rounded with no obvious snout; tall, triangular dorsal fin, up to 6 ft (1.8 m) high in male; broad, rounded flippers; tail black on top, white on underside

Habits Social, living in a tight-knit family group or "pod"; fast, active swimmer; acrobatic at the surface, will breach, spy-hop, and tail slap

Breeding Single calf born about every 8 years after gestation period of 17 months. Weaned at 14–18 months; sexually mature at 12–16 years. Males may live 35–60 years, females up to 90 years in the wild; rarely survives more than a few years in captivity

Basic description of animal, its life, and distribution

Voice Varied, including complex, often pulsed, calls

Diet Ssmall fish and squid to seals, turtles, seabirds, and even other whales

Habitat Open sea to coastal waters; estuaries; often around ice floes in polar waters

Distribution Every ocean in the world, from polar regions to equator

Status Population: 100,000; IUCN Lower Risk: conservation dependent; CITES II. Widespread and quite numerous

Conservation status if threatened (see Glossary)

Locator maps showing each animal's normal range

Article describes a particular animal

Scientific name of animal

Captions to photographs provide additional information about each animal's lifestyle

Common name of animal

LARGE CARNIVORES

Panthera tigris

Tiger

The tiger, with its black-and-orange striped coat, is one of the most distinctive of all mammals. It is feared the world over, but nowadays the species is severely reduced in numbers.

IN MANY WAYS THE TIGER IS MORE deserving of the title King of Beasts than its close cousin, the lion. It is the largest of all the cats, and its range once extended from the fringes of Europe eastward to Russia's Sea of Okhotsk and south to the Indonesian islands of Java and Bali. Tigers from different parts of this vast range differ considerably, so the species has been divided into eight subspecies. They are named after the region in which they occur, but most can also be distinguished by their appearance. For example, Siberian tigers are consistently bigger than other subspecies, with males weighing up to 660 pounds (300 kg). This almost certainly makes them the biggest cats ever to have lived, including huge extinct species such as the saber-toothed tiger and the cave lion.

Common name Tiger

Scientific name *Panthera tigris*

Family Felidae

Order Carnivora

Size Length head/body: 4.6–9 ft (1.4–2.7 m); tail length: 23–43 in (60–110 cm); height at shoulder: 31–43 in (80–110 cm)

Weight Male 143–364 lb (65–165 kg); female 143–364 lb (90–300 kg)

Key features Huge, highly muscular cat with large head and long tail; unmistakable orange coat with dark stripes; underside white

Habits Solitary and highly territorial; active mostly at night; climbs and swims well

Breeding Litters of 1–6 (usually 2 or 3) cubs born at any time of year after gestation period of 95–110 days. Weaned at 3–6 months; females sexually mature at 3–4 years, males at 4–5 years. May live up to 26 years in captivity, rarely more than 10 in the wild

Voice Purrs, grunts, and blood-curdling roars

Diet Mainly large, hoofed mammals, including deer, buffalo, antelope, and gaur

Habitat Tropical forests and swamps, grasslands with good vegetation cover and water nearby

Distribution India, Bhutan, Bangladesh, Nepal, China; southeastern Siberia; Myanmar (Burma), Vietnam, Laos, Thailand, and Sumatra

Status Population: 5,000–7,500; IUCN Endangered; CITES I. Previously hunted for fur and body parts, and to protect people and livestock

▶ A Bengal tiger wades through water. Tigers are proficient swimmers and can cross rivers that are 4 to 5 miles (7 to 8 km) wide without difficulty.

▶ Juvenile tigers are fond of play fighting, like the two below.

Different Adaptations

The smallest tigers came from Bali and rarely exceeded 220 pounds (100 kg) in weight. They are now probably extinct. As a general rule, body size relates to the climate and the type of prey available in different parts of the tiger's range. Siberian tigers need to cope with intensely cold and snowy winters, and specialize in catching large prey such as cattle and deer. In contrast, tigers in Indonesia inhabit tropical jungle where overheating is a serious problem for large animals, and the favored prey includes pigs and small deer. The Chinese tiger is thought to be the ancestor of the other types. Fossils show that tigers first appeared in China about 2 million years ago, and they spread north, south, and west from there. Modern Chinese tigers have several traits that zoologists consider rather primitive, including a shortened skull and relatively close-set eyes.

Easy-to-read and comprehensive text

20

familiar with specific animals in the context of their evolutionary history and biological relationships.

A number of other features presents you with helpful extra information. In each volume you will find a detailed list of the species within each family covered in the volume. You will also find a **Glossary** that will help you if there are words in the text that you do not fully understand. Each volume includes a list of useful **Websites** that help you take your research further.

Who's Who tables summarize classification of each major group

Introductory article describes major groups of animals

SMALL CARNIVORES

At-a-glance boxes cover topics of special interest

Graphic full-color photographs bring text to life

The Disappearing Tiger

Detailed maps clarify points described in text

Meticulous drawings illustrate a typical selection of group members

Introductory article describes family or closely related groups

LARGE CARNIVORES

The Hyena Family

Tables summarize classification of groups and give examples of animals in the groups. They also list the total number of genera and species in each group

THE HYENA FAMILY

Animal Families

Each volume of *Ultimate Wildlife* features animal species that are grouped together because they share similar characteristics. The first volumes are about mammals, and this volume focuses on cattle, sheep, goats, and antelope. The volumes are arranged in order to collect together the animals into the categories that are recognized by scientists.

The Animal Kingdom

The living world is divided into five kingdoms, and animals (Animalia) make up one of those kingdoms.

The other kingdoms are Plantae (plants), Fungi, Protista (single-celled life-forms, including algae) and Monera (which includes bacteria). The animal kingdom is divided into numerous major groups called phyla, but only one of them (Chordata) contains those animals that have a backbone. Chordates, or vertebrates, as they are popularly known, include all the animals familiar to us and those most studied by scientists – mammals, birds, fish, reptiles, and amphibians. In all, there are at least 38,000 species of vertebrates, while the phyla that contain animals without backbones (invertebrates, such as insects and spiders) include several million species, probably many more.

Mammals in particular

The volumes on mammals focus on the most familiar of animals, those most easily recognized as having fur (although this is absent in many sea mammals, such as the whales and dolphins) and that provide milk for their young. Mammals are divided into major groups (carnivores, primates, rodents, and marsupials, to name just a few). All the major groups are shown on the diagram, left. So, for example, you can see that

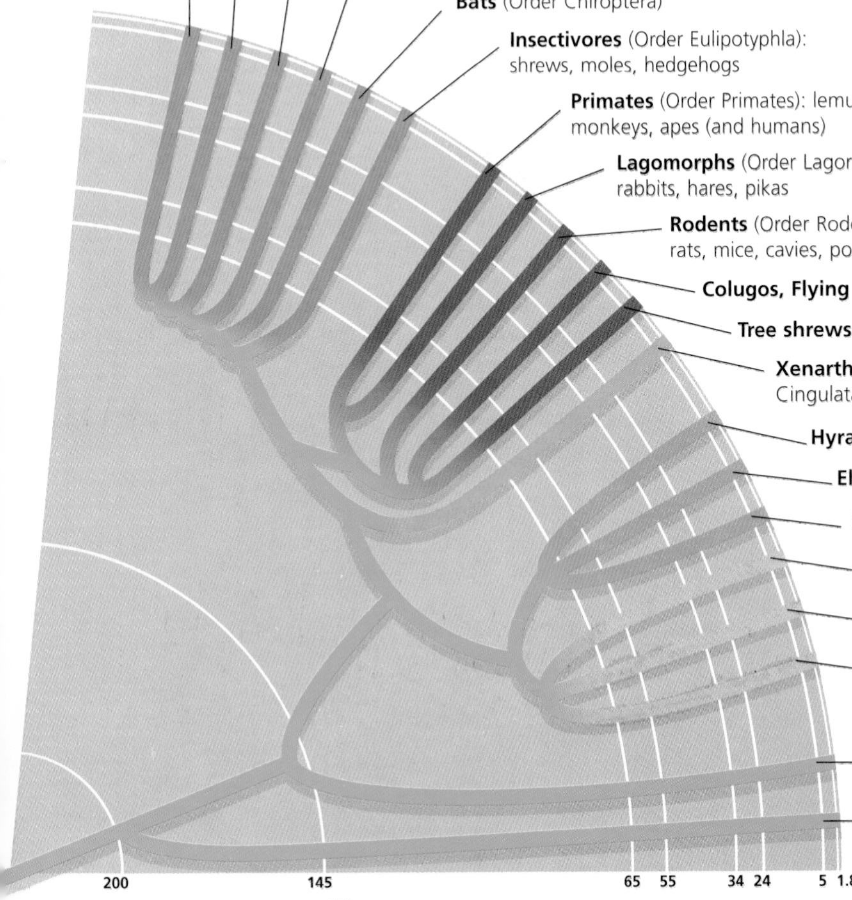

The chart shows the major groups of mammals, arranged in evolutionary relationship.

Carnivores (Order Carnivora): raccoons, weasels, otters, skunks, cats, dogs, bears, hyenas, seals, sea lions

Pangolins (Order Pholidota)

Odd-toed ungulates (Order Perissodactyla): horses, rhinoceroses, tapirs

Whales, dolphins, and Even-toed ungulates (Order Cetartiodactyla)

Bats (Order Chiroptera)

Insectivores (Order Eulipotyphla): shrews, moles, hedgehogs

Primates (Order Primates): lemurs, monkeys, apes (and humans)

Lagomorphs (Order Lagormorpha): rabbits, hares, pikas

Rodents (Order Rodentia): squirrels, rats, mice, cavies, porcupines

Colugos, Flying lemurs (Order Dermoptera)

Tree shrews (Order Scandentia)

Xenarthrans (Orders Pilosa and Cingulata): anteaters, sloths, armadillos

Hyraxes (Order Hyracoidea)

Elephants (Order Proboscidea)

Dugongs, manatees (Order Sirenia)

Aardvark (Order Tubulidentata)

Sengis (Order Macroscelidea)

Tenrecs and Golden moles (Order Afrosoricida)

Marsupials (Supercohort: Marsupialia, contains several Orders): opossums, kangaroos, koala

Monotremes (Order Monotremata): platypus, echidnas

| 200 | 145 | 65 | 55 | 34 | 24 | 5 | 1.8 |

million years ago

The main groups of animals

```
                    ANIMALS
                  Kingdom Animalia
                         |
         ┌───────────────┴───────────────┐
   Vertebrates/                      Invertebrates
    Chordates                        Numerous phyla
  Phylum Chordata
         |
 ┌───────┬───────┬───────┬───────┐
Mammals  Birds  Reptiles Amphibians  Fish    Insects, spiders,
Class   Class   Class    Class    Several    mollusks, worms,
Mammalia Aves   Reptilia Amphibia  classes   shrimps, etc
```

The main groups of animals alive today. Each kingdom is divided into phyla, and within each phylum there are many classes.

seals and sea lions followed a very similar evolution to the carnivores until relatively recently (in evolutionary terms).

Naming Mammals

To be able to discuss animals, names are needed for the different kinds. Most people regard tigers as one kind of animal and lions as another. All tigers look more or less alike. They breed together and produce young like themselves. This popular distinction between kinds of animals corresponds closely to the zoologists' distinction between species. All tigers belong to one species and all lions to another. The lion species has different names in different languages (for example, *Löwe* in German, *Simba* in Swahili), and often a single species may have several common names. For example, the North American mountian lion is also known as the cougar, puma, panther, and catamount.

Zoologists find it convenient to have internationally recognized names for species and use a standardized system of two-word Latin names. The lion is called *Panthera leo* and the tiger *Panthera tigris*. The first word, *Panthera*, is the name of the genus (a group of closely similar species), which includes the lion and the tiger. The second word, *leo* or *tigris*, indicates the particular species within the genus. Scientific names are recognized all over the world. The scientific name is used whatever the language, even when the alphabet is different, as in Chinese or Russian. The convention allows for precision and helps avoid most confusion. However, it is also common for one species to apparently have more that one scientific name. That can be because a particular species may have been described and named at different times without the zoologists knowing it was one species.

It is often necessary to make statements about larger groups of animals: for example, all the catlike animals or all the mammals. A formal system of classification makes this possible. Domestic cats are similar to lions and tigers, but not as similar as those species are to each other (for example, they do not roar). They are put in a different genus (*Felis*), but *Felis*, *Panthera*, and other catlike animals are all grouped together as the family Felidae. The flesh-eating mammals (cats, dogs, hyenas, weasels, and so on), together with a few plant-eaters that are obviously related to them (such as pandas), are grouped in the order Carnivora. These and all the other animals that suckle their young are grouped in the class Mammalia. Finally, the mammals are included, with all other animals that have backbones (fish, amphibians, reptiles, and birds) and some other animals that seem to be related to them, in the phylum Chordata.

Rank	Scientific name	Common name
Phylum	Chordata	Animals with a backbone
Class	Mammalia	All mammals
Order	Carnivora	Flesh-eaters/carnivores
Family	Felidae	All cats
Genus	*Panthera*	Big cats
Species	*leo*	Lion

The kingdom Animalia is subdivided into groups such as classes, families, genera, and species. Above is the classification of the lion.

Cattle, Sheep, Goats, and Antelope

Cattle, sheep, goats, and antelope (the family Bovidae) are a highly successful family of mammals. They now inhabit every continent except Antarctica and have developed into an amazing diversity of species. They come in a wide range of body forms and sizes, from the tiny pygmy antelope, which is not much larger than a rabbit, to the African buffalo and American bison, which can be 6.5 feet (2 m) tall.

Where Do Bovids Live?

Bovids are primarily an Old World group, found throughout Africa and most of Eurasia, but some are also native to North America and even certain islands in the Arctic and East Indies. Some have been introduced to New Guinea, New Zealand, South America, Australia, and South Georgia, and domesticated species have accompanied humans over most of the globe. Most species live in dry, open habitats, such as grasslands, scrub, or desert, but some live in forests, swamps, or even on the arctic tundra. Although they are all herbivores, the animals have a range of feeding styles and preferences, from grazing grass to browsing trees. By specializing on different types of plants, and on fresh new growth or tough mature leaves, and feeding at different heights, many species coexist in one habitat without competing directly for food.

↰ *Horn and antler shape and composition have evolved differently in the families Giraffidae, Cervidae, and Bovidae: giraffe (1); roe deer (2); pronghorn (3); and common eland (4).*

▨ bone	▨ deciduous bone
▨ keratin (horn)	▨ deciduous keratin (horn)

The ancestors of these ungulate families lived in Africa and Eurasia. Their original geographical distribution is reflected in their current centers of abundance and diversity—in the grasslands and savannas of tropical Africa and southern and central Asia. Here they evolved from small, hornless ruminants. They reached their peak of diversity in Africa during the late Pliocene epoch (about 2 to 3 million years ago) and reached North America during the Pleistocene about 1 million years ago. However, they were never native to South America; the first bovids there were the livestock brought in by the Spanish conquistadors.

Characteristic Horns

Antelope, cattle, sheep, and goats all have horns—a central bony core that is part of the skull. The bone is usually covered with a tough sheath made of keratin (the same substance that forms fingernails and claws). Horns are unbranched and permanent: They are not shed every year as happens with the antlers of deer. Males always have horns, and so do the females in some species, although they are often smaller than in the males. Horns may form a sweeping curve, coiled spirals, or straight spikes. There is usually a single pair of horns located on the front of the head behind the eyes. Four-horned antelope have an additional pair of smaller horns above the eyes. In the

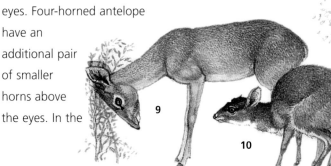

⤴ *Species of dwarf antelope and gazelles: klipspringer
(1); beira (2); dibatag (3); springbok (4); goitered gazelle (5); Tibetan gazelle (6);
slender-horned gazelle (7); dama gazelle (8); Kirk's dik-dik (9); royal antelope (10);
oribi (11); steenbok (12); and blackbuck (13).*

Subfamily Bovinae (wild cattle, spiral-horned, and four-horned antelope): 9 genera, at least 24 species

Bubalus 4 species, including lowland anoa (*B. depressicornis*); tamaraw (*B. mindorensis*)

Bos 5 species, including banteng (*B. javanicus*); gaur (*B. frontalis*)

Pseudoryx 1 species, saola (*P. nghetinhensis*)

Syncerus 1 species, African buffalo (*S. caffer*)

Bison 2 species, American bison (*B. bison*); European bison (*B. bonasus*)

Tragelaphus 7 species, including bushbuck (*T. scriptus*); mountain nyala (*T. buxtoni*)

Taurotragus 2 species, common eland (*T. oryx*); giant eland (*T. derbianus*)

Tetracerus 1 species, four-horned antelope (*T. quadricornis*)

Boselaphus 1 species, nilgai (*B. tragocamelus*)

Subfamily Cephalophinae (duikers): 2 genera, 18 species

Cephalophus 17 species, including blue duiker (*C. monticola*); bay duiker (*C. dorsalis*)

Some species within the *Cephalophus* genus may belong to a separate genus, *Philantomba*

Sylvicapra 1 species, common duiker (*S. grimmia*)

Subfamily Reduncinae 3 genera, 9 species

Kobus 5 species, including waterbuck (*K. ellipsiprymnus*); kob (*K. kob*)

Pelea 1 species, Gray roebuck (*P. capreolus*)

Redunca 3 species, including southern reedbuck (*R.arundinum*)

Subfamily Aepycerotinae 1 genus, 1 species

Aepyceros 1 species, impala (*A. melampus*)

Subfamily Alcelaphinae 4 genera, 8 species

Alcelaphus 2 species, including hartebeest (*A. buselaphus*)

Beatragus 1 species, hirola or Hunter's hartebeest (*B. hunteri*)

Connochaetes 2 species, black wildebeest (*C. gnou*) and blue wildebeest or brindled gnu (*C. taurinus*)

Damaliscus 3 species, including bontebuck (*A. buselaphus*)

Subfamily Hippotraginae (grazing antelopes): 3 genera, 7 species

Hippotragus 2 species, roan antelope (*H. equinus*); sable antelope (*H. niger*)

Oryx 4 species, including scimitar-horned oryx (*O. dammah*); gemsbok (*O. gazella*); Arabian oryx (*O. leucoryx*)

Addax 1 species, addax (*A. nasomaculatus*)

Subfamily Antelopinae (gazelles, dwarf antelope): 13 genera, 33 species

Gazella 10 species, including goitered gazelle (*G. subguttarosa*); dama gazelle (*G. dama*); slender-horned gazelle (*G. leptoceros*)

Some species within the *Gazella* genus may belong to a separate genus, *Nanger*

Antilope 1 species, blackbuck (*A. cervicapra*)

Eudorcas 2 species, including Thomson's gazelle (*E.thomsonii*)

Procapra 3 species, including Tibetan gazelle (*P. picticaudata*)

Antidorcas 1 species, springbok (*A. marsupialis*)

Ammodorcas 1 species, dibatag (*A. clarkei*)

Litocranius 1 species, gerenuk (*L. walleri*)

Neotragus 3 species, including royal antelope (*N. pygmaeus*); pygmy antelope (*N. batesi*)

Madoqua 4 species, Salt's dik-dik (*M. saltiana*); Kirk's dik-dik (*M. kirkii*)

Oreotragus 1 species, klipspringer (*O. oreotragus*)

Raphicerus 3 species, including steenbok (*R. campestris*)

Ourebia 1 species, oribi (*O. ourebi*)

Dorcatragus 1 species, beira (*D. megalotis*)

Saiga 1 species, saiga (*S. tatarica*)

Subfamily Caprinae (goat antelope): 12 genera, 33 species

Hemitragus 3 species, including Himalayan tahr (*H. jemlahicus*)

Ammotragus 1 species, barbary sheep (*A. lervia*)

Pseudois 1 species, blue sheep (*P. nayaur*)

Capra 9 species, including wild goat (*C. aegagrus*); ibex (*C. ibex*), Spanish goat or ibex (*C. pyrenaica*)

Ovis 6 species, including domestic sheep (*O. aries*); mouflon (*O. musimon*)

Capricornis 6 species, including mainland serow (*C. sumatraensis*); Japanese serow (*C. crispus*)

Nemorhaedus 1 species, goral (*N. goral*)

Rupicapra 2 species, chamois (*R. rupicapra*); Pyrenean chamois (*R. pyrenaica*)

Oreamnos 1 species, mountain goat (*O. americanus*)

Budorcas 1 species, takin (*B. taxicolor*)

Ovibos 1 species, muskox (*O. moschatus*)

Pantholops 1 species, chiru or Tibetan antelope (*P. hodgsoni*)

Family Antilocapridae: 1 genus, 1 species

Antilocapra pronghorn (*A. americana*)

pronghorn (family Antilocapridae) the structure of the horn is unique: It has a bony core, but the keratin sheath around it is shed every year. It also has a branched tip.

Most antelope live in Africa, where they account for almost all of the species in the family Bovidae living there. Their success is partly due to their ability to cope with arid conditions. They conserve water by not sweating, recycling urea, concentrating their urine, and absorbing nearly all the water from their feces. They can cope with an increase in body temperature of up to 11°F (6°C).

Hunting and Domestication

Most of the world's game species are bovids, and many millions have been hunted for their meat, hides, and for sport. Hunting has driven the South African bluebuck (*Hippotragus leucophaeus*) to extinction, and many more species are now rare or threatened. However, humans do not always have a negative impact. Cattle, goats, and sheep are far more common than they would have been had they not been domesticated. There are now around 1.2 billion domestic cattle, over a billion sheep, and around 445 million goats worldwide.

Sheep and goats were the first bovids to be domesticated. The process first happened in the Middle East, around 7,500 BC or earlier. Domestic goats are almost certainly descended from wild goats. Domestic sheep probably originated from the mouflon, which is the only wild sheep to share the same number of chromosomes. The thick fleecy coat of modern sheep is a result of selective breeding—the coat of wild sheep has coarse hairs, lost in modern varieties.

At a later date cattle were domesticated from a large-horned wild ancestor called the aurochs. The aurochs was once widespread throughout Eurasia, but has been extinct

⊙ Orkney Island Sohay sheep—from the Scottish island of Orkney—are a subspecies of the domestic sheep. They descended from mouflonlike animals about 10,000 years ago.

An Outsider: the American Pronghorn Antelope

Most of the animals in this group of mammals belong to the family Bovidae. The other family included here is the Antilocapridae, which today has only one living species—the pronghorn. The ruminant ancestors of the Antilocapridae reached North America in the early Miocene, where they diversified into a large number of species. Most of them died out at the end of the Pleistocene, probably from a combination of climate change and hunting by early human colonizers.

A male pronghorn. The pronghorn belongs to its own family of antelope and is the only living antelope species to naturally inhabit the American continent.

in the wild since 1627. It is likely that cattle were domesticated independently in different parts of the world. European-type humpless cattle are widespread in temperate regions, while the humped zebu cattle live in tropical regions. In early cultures oxen were a source of power used for pulling carts and later plows. As crop growing developed alongside the domestication of bovids, human life changed dramatically. Settlement and farming cultures spread throughout the world, and sheep and cattle were transported to many countries where they had not previously existed. The biological success of our own species owes much to our partnership with bovids.

Common name American bison (buffalo)

Scientific name *Bison bison*

Family Bovidae

Order Artiodactyla

Size Length head/body: male 10–12 ft (3–3.8 m); female 7–10 ft (2.1–3.2 m); tail length: 17–35 in (43–90 cm); height at shoulder: up to 6.2 ft (1.9 m)

Weight Male 1,000–2,000 lb (454–907 kg); female 790–1,200 lb (358–544 kg)

Key features Large, oxlike animal with head held low and large hump over the shoulders; forelegs, neck, and shoulders covered in long, dark-brown hair; horns present in both sexes

Habits Lives in large herds that migrate across open grasslands; feeds mostly early and late in day

Breeding Single calf born May–August after gestation period of 9–10 months. Weaned at about 6 months; sexually mature at 2–3 years. May live up to 40 years in captivity, up to 25 in the wild

Voice Snorts, grunts, and cowlike noises; bulls bellow and roar during the rut

Diet Mostly grass; also sedges, wild flowers, and shrubs such as willow, birch, and sagebrush; lichens and mosses in winter

Habitat Prairies, sagebrush, and open wooded areas

Distribution Midwestern U.S. and Canada

Status Population: about 30,000 in conservation herds, 500,000 in commercial herds; IUCN Near Threatened; CITES II

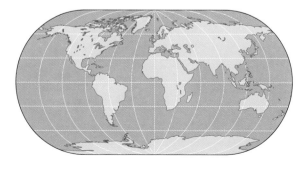

American Bison

Bison bison

The fate of the American bison demonstrates one of the worst examples of ruthless exploitation, which reduced the animal to the point of extinction. Conversely, it is also one of the best examples of successful conservation management.

THE BISON IS THE BIGGEST ANIMAL to have roamed the North American continent in historic times. Scientists know it by this name, but to most Americans it is more familiar as the buffalo. The two names apply to the same animal, and confusion arises as an accident of history. A similar problem applies to the use of the word "Indian" in reference to the native people of North America. Logically, Indians come from India, not America, but European explorers meeting these people for the first time called them Indians to differentiate them from white men like themselves. Similarly, when the bison was first discovered by European explorers, they sometimes called it "buffalo" because it reminded them of the water buffalo—a species that was domesticated in Asia hundreds of years ago. It was also rather similar to the African buffalo. They were the nearest familiar creatures to the newfound bison of North America. The terms "Indian" and "buffalo" have continued to be widely used to this day.

Dangers from Humans

Huge herds of bison used to roam the open plains and lightly wooded areas of central North America. It is claimed that the total population may have numbered up to 50 million animals, but they were slaughtered mercilessly by the spreading human population. As a result of such actions, the bison had already become extinct east of the Mississippi River by the early 19th century. As ranching and settlement steadily expanded westward in the United States, the bison's decline may also have been hastened by diseases caught from domestic

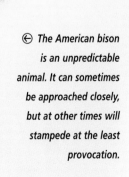

cattle, to which the wild species was not resistant. In the Midwest commercial hunting for hides and meat resulted in massive slaughter. The coming of the railroads not only created a market for meat, but also made it possible to export meat, hides, and bones to distant buyers, increasing the pressure on the herds.

Wasteful Executions

Professional hunters like "Buffalo Bill" Cody were engaged to supply railway workers with food, and many of them killed several thousand buffalo each year. The hunting was exceedingly wasteful, since often only the skins were taken. Sometimes just the tongues were collected, the rest of the meat being left on the prairie to rot, since it was not valuable enough to warrant the cost of transporting it elsewhere. Some animals were shot from moving trains for target practice and never used at all. For every bison skin that actually reached the market, at least three other animals were often wasted. An English traveler in 1873 counted 67 carcasses at one spot where hunters had shot buffalo coming to drink along the Arkansas River. An army colonel counted 112 bodies within a 200-yard (183-m) radius, all shot by one man from the same spot in 45 minutes.

Railroad Casualties

The transcontinental railroad also split the bison herd in two, making two smaller populations and also making it easier to gain access to the animals. As late as 1870 there were still 4 to 5 million buffalo to the north and plenty more to the south. Today it is difficult to believe that so many large animals ever roamed the American plains, and people assume stories told about "millions of buffalo" must surely be

The American bison is an unpredictable animal. It can sometimes be approached closely, but at other times will stampede at the least provocation.

exaggerations. However, there is documentary evidence proving that there were indeed enormous numbers killed. For example, fur company records show more than 35,000 bison skins being shipped from Fort Benton in 1857 alone. The Santa Fe Railroad carried over 1.3 million hides in just three years (1872 to 1874). In the north the manager of the Northern Pacific Railroad reported that his company had transported 30,000 to 40,000 skins each year in the late 1870s from Bismarck, North Dakota. In 1881 the quantities reached over 75,000. But within 10 years the trade had virtually collapsed, reflecting the almost total extermination of the bison.

Bison Census

A census in 1887 found only 541 bison left on the prairies. Conservation efforts, led by W. T. Hornaday, established captive herds in Montana and Oklahoma, and the bison has not looked back since. Today bison roam widely on the American prairies and in the sagebrush country of Wyoming. There are also large herds in South Dakota and on many private ranches. The only place where a wild population has always remained is Yellowstone National Park. About 1,500 animals live there, but sometimes range outside the park, where they damage crops and perhaps also spread disease to cattle.

European Bison

The European bison (*Bison bonasus*) is Europe's largest land animal and looks like its American cousin, but is taller and more slender in appearance. It is bigger than an ox, with a short, thick, hairy neck. The humped shoulders are less pronounced than in the American species, and the head is held higher. European bison are forest-edge inhabitants, coming out to graze in the open, where they eat about 65 pounds (30 kg) of grass per day. They also eat leaves and bark. In winter they are often given additional food to help their survival. The bison live in small herds of up to 20 animals. Their rutting season extends from August until October, and a single calf is born between May and July. Calves are fed by their mother for up to a year, and they can live to be more than 25 years old.

The species used to occur widely in the forests of Europe, but was brought to the brink of extinction by habitat loss and excessive hunting. By the 19th century only two populations remained, one in Poland and the other in the Caucasus Mountains of southeastern Europe. Both were wiped out early in the 20th century as a result of poaching. About 50 bison remained in various parks and zoos. Enough animals were bred from them to support reintroductions to the wild. The total number of European bison now exceeds 3,000, distributed among more than 20 wild populations and over 200 parks and zoos.

⊕ *A herd of bison graze in Yellowstone National Park—the only place where wild herds have lived continually.*

Protected from hunters and predators, bison numbers have steadily increased, and by 1995 the total population was about 150,000— almost 90 percent of them on privately owned ranches. The herds now need to be culled annually to avoid the animals becoming too numerous for their food supply to support.

Bison meat has high market value, being tasty and low in fat, and many cattle ranchers keep bison as a commercial venture.

Slow Grazers

Bison are essentially grazing animals, living in large herds on the short-grass prairies, but also in lightly wooded areas. They are active during the day and also at night. They generally spend their time moving slowly, grazing as they go. They cover a mile or two (about 3 km) each day. In the past they would migrate long distances to fresh feeding areas, but that is rarely possible now, since almost all the modern herds live within enclosed areas.

Nevertheless, where there is room to do so (in Yellowstone National Park, for example), the bison still move seasonally from the high ground where they spend the summers to richer pastures on lower ground in the fall. Bison normally spend much of their time resting, but they also like to wallow in dust or mud and rub themselves against fence posts, boulders, and trees. They have acute senses of hearing and smell. Despite their large size and

rather ungainly appearance, they can run at speeds of nearly 40 miles per hour (64 km/h)—at least for short distances. They are also capable of swimming across large rivers. Bison herds are normally composed of a few dozen animals, although in the past many thousands might occur in the same area. Mature males travel alone or in small groups for most of the year and join with the females for the summer breeding season.

During the rut, in July and August, dominant males fight fiercely by butting each other head to head. They make a lot of noise at that time of year, bellowing and roaring to establish status—sounds that can sometimes be heard miles away. Successful males stay close to receptive females for several days until they are able to mate with them, meanwhile keeping rival males away. A single calf is born after about 10 months—twins are very rare. The young animals become capable of breeding

⬆ *Two European bison bulls sparring. The rutting season in European bison is from August to October, with one calf born between May and July. These bison are Europe's largest land animals—taller and more slender than their American cousins.*

from the age of about two years, but there seems to be a geographical variation in breeding success. In Oklahoma about two-thirds of the adult females may be found breeding each year, but more than three-quarters of females do so in Montana. Females can produce a calf every year but sometimes miss a year, allowing time to build up their body reserves before becoming pregnant again.

Little to Fear

Newborn calves weigh about 35 to 70 pounds (16 to 32 kg). They can run after three hours and are weaned by the time they are one year old. The mother guards her calf jealously and will chase away predators and other intruders. Wild bison have little to fear these days now that wolves and other large predators are scarce. They are the biggest land mammals in the Western Hemisphere, and many will live to be 20 years old unless they are culled by herd managers or licensed hunters.

A smaller type of bison known as the wood bison (*Bison bison athabascae*) occurs in wooded areas of southwestern Canada, and is often treated as though it were a different species. It has been listed as Threatened by Canadian conservation authorities. However, DNA analysis suggests that the wood bison is in fact not a separate species, merely a smaller northern race.

⊕ *A herd of bison stampeding across the prairies is an awe-inspiring sight. The bison were once found in vast numbers, but hunting brought them to the brink of extinction. Now they are no longer threatened.*

A Keystone Species

The bison was once the dominant factor in the ecology of the North American continent. Its grazing helped maintain short-grass prairies in a condition that was suitable for many plains species of birds, reptiles, and plants that were unable to thrive where the grass grew taller. Bison are among the natural prey of cougars and wolves. The remains of their carcasses fed scavengers, and their molted fur was eagerly collected by nesting birds. Some Native American people depended heavily on the bison herds for meat, hides, and many other useful products. The skins were used to make weatherproof tents and clothing sewn with lengths of bison sinew. Hair was used for bedding, and bones were carved into ornaments and tools. The bison supported a whole community of plants and animals within which it lived. Removing these vital creatures from the scene disrupts the whole ecosystem, just as removing the keystone from the center of the arch of a bridge will cause it to collapse. For a while it was even official policy to remove bison in an effort to undermine Native American communities during the westward colonization of North America.

Two elderly Native American women photographed in the 1950s clad in buffalo-skin capes. Some Native Americans were heavily dependent on the buffalo.

Common name African buffalo

Scientific name *Syncerus caffer*

Family	Bovidae
Order	Artiodactyla
Size	Length head/body: 8–11 ft (2.4–3.4 m); tail length: 30–43 in (75–110 cm); height at shoulder: 4.6–5.5 ft (1.4–1.7 m)

Weight 550–1,870 lb (250–848 kg). Male more heavily built than female

Key features	Huge black or brown oxlike creature with hairy ears and massive horns that meet on top of the forehead to form a heavy "boss"; reddish forest form is smaller
Habits	Lives in herds, sometimes of only a few animals, but many hundreds may congregate seasonally in good feeding areas
Breeding	One calf normally produced every 2 years after gestation period of 11 months. Weaned at about 1 year; sexually mature at 3–5 years. May live over 29 years in captivity, 18 in the wild
Voice	Generally silent
Diet	Grass; wide variety of swamp vegetation
Habitat	Savanna woodland and open grassy glades; usually near water and often wallows in mud; forest form lives under continuous tree cover
Distribution	Widely dispersed across West, central, and East Africa south of Sahara
Status	Population: probably at least 500,000; IUCN Least Concern. Generally common, although severely reduced in places due to disease, habitat loss, and hunting

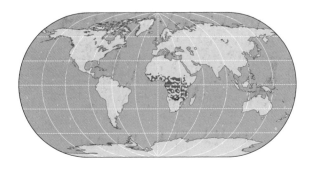

African Buffalo *Syncerus caffer*

Grazing quietly in large herds, the African buffalo belies its reputation for ferocity and unpredictability. It is probably still the most abundant and widespread of all the African "big game" animals despite serious losses in the past.

THE AFRICAN BUFFALO IS FOUND in grassy savanna areas across much of Africa south of the Sahara Desert. In the west of the continent there is a small brownish form that occurs mainly in forest areas. The forest buffalo may be only half the size of some eastern specimens, and it is often a bright chestnut color. It has sometimes been regarded as a different species, but is generally considered to be just a smaller variant of the common buffalo.

Typical Features

Buffalo are typically large black creatures, with a deep chest, stocky limbs, and a heavy head. They have big ears that droop downward and have fringes of long hairs. Buffalo also have massive horns that are present in both sexes. The horns meet at the base to form a thick protective shield on top of the head. They can be up to 5 feet (1.5 m) across, but are usually more compact. They curve downward, then up again to end in sharp points. Female buffalo are generally smaller than males—some of which can become really massive animals.

Old bulls often lose most of their sparse hair, exposing a grayish skin. Their color also depends on what sort of mud or dust they have been wallowing in recently. Wallowing is a popular activity, especially in hot weather, and the African buffalo is rarely found far from water. Wet places also offer abundant food in the form of lush grass and a wide variety of marsh plants. Such places often attract very

⤒ *A male African buffalo displaying the huge horns that are present in both sexes. The horns curve downward, then back up to end in a sharp point.*

large herds of buffalo, sometimes numbering several hundred animals. Big herds are especially common in the dry season, when food is less attractive elsewhere.

Buffalo tend to remain in the same herd and in much the same area throughout their life. A herd may have a home range as small as 4 square miles (10 sq. km), although in dry habitats the animals range more widely. A herd will frequently move between favorite feeding places, but the total distance covered will normally be less than about 100 miles (160 km) in a year. Moving around spreads the grazing impact over a wider area than if they stayed in the same place all the time. This is important, since buffalo are large animals and eat a lot each day. The animals plod around slowly,

moving at only 2 or 3 miles per hour (3 to 5 km/h), grazing and resting alternately. They usually drink in the morning and evening, and rest during the hottest part of the day. The animals will become nocturnal if they are disturbed as a result of human activity.

The African buffalo is a grazing animal, eating mainly grass, but it occasionally browses small shrubs. It is also a wary creature with extremely sensitive hearing. Animals will stop feeding and raise their heads in response to even the smallest unfamiliar sound. By contrast, their vision is relatively poor.

Follow the Leader

Buffalo herds consist of social groups, each of which is built around females with their young from previous years. Groups of bachelor males are also included within the larger herd. Herds have only a very loose structure, and there is rarely a single herd leader. When the herd moves on, the actual leading animal may be either a male or a female and often changes as

19

animals stop to feed. Older males often segregate and may live alone or in small groups. In some areas buffalo breed throughout the year, but normally breeding is linked to the timing of the rains, which varies throughout the different parts of Africa.

When the cows are ready to mate, the bulls take a close interest in them and compete for mating opportunities. They establish a rank order based on size and strength—sometimes coming to blows before dominance is established. A single reddish or black calf is born after a gestation period of around 11 months. It weighs about 100 pounds (45 kg) at birth and stays close to its mother for two years or more. Small buffalo enjoy relative safety within the herd, where there are always a number of individuals on the lookout for danger. The large adults are sufficiently powerful that they can keep predators such as leopards at bay, and the young buffalo have little to fear unless they are caught in the open by attacking lions, for example.

The forest buffalo is similar in its habits, except that it spends more time among shady forest cover. Moreover, the forest buffalo do not form large herds, and groups of more than about 20 are relatively unusual. In West Africa, the main home of forest buffalo, human use of the land tends to be intensive and increasing, so the forest buffalo there are often under greater pressure than their savanna-dwelling relatives in the eastern half of the continent. Populations of forest buffalo are now fragmented, especially where large areas of forest have been taken over for human use.

Victims of Hunting

Buffalo were hunted extensively for food and for sport. They are frequent victims of wire snares, too, set by poachers to catch "bush meat." Buffalo are generally quiet, placid creatures, but can be bad tempered and unpredictable, especially if they become wounded. That has led to the animal having a reputation for attacking people without

⬇ A herd of buffalo drinking at a water hole. Herds of many hundreds may congregate seasonally in good feeding areas.

Buffalos and Birds

Wet areas favored by the buffalo are also frequented by cattle egrets (*Bubulcus ibis*). The white-plumaged birds like to stalk around among mammal herds to catch the frogs and insects that the animals disturb. The birds are often seen in association with the African buffalo.

Oxpeckers (*Buphagus africanus*) are another bird associated with buffalo. They climb around on the animal's thick skin, picking off parasites and feeding from small oozing wounds. Their chittering alarm calls warn the buffalo of approaching danger. A partnership between different animals that both derive benefit from is called symbiosis.

apparent provocation. There are even reports of buffalo attacking and killing lions. Their large size makes charging buffalo extremely dangerous animals, since they pursue people on foot. Among big-game hunters the buffalo was considered the meanest of creatures, to be treated with the greatest caution. Many hunters feared the buffalo more than even lions or leopards, especially if a wounded animal had to be followed on foot in dense scrub.

Declining Numbers

Rinderpest, a disease of cattle, swept through the buffalo population in southern Africa in the 1890s, causing local extinctions. Even where some animals survived, their numbers were severely reduced and had still not recovered fully a century later. Hunting and disease have also caused buffalo numbers to decline in many areas. Nevertheless, overall the species remains fairly abundant, especially in national parks and other protected areas, and is not considered to be threatened. Loss of wetland habitat to farming is likely to be the principal threat faced by the African buffalo in the future.

⊕ Egrets, often seen in association with buffalo, like to feed on frogs and insects that the animals disturb. Their alarm calls warn the buffalo of potential danger.

Common name Yak

Scientific name *Bos grunniens* (*B. mutus*)

Family Bovidae

Order Artiodactyla

Size Length head/body: up to 11 ft (3.3 m); tail length: about 20 in (50 cm); height at shoulder: up to 6.6 ft (2 m)

        Weight Male 670–2,200 lb (300–1,000 kg). Female about 60% smaller

Key features Massive, shaggy, oxlike animal with high, humped shoulders and low-slung head; dense woolly hair—almost reaching ground; dark brown to black with white around muzzle; both sexes have curved horns about 47–78 in (120–200 cm) long

Habits Lives in small herds, gathering into larger groups in summer where food is available

Breeding Single calf born in June every other year after gestation period of 255–304 days. Weaned at 1 year; sexually mature at 6–8 years. May live up to 25 years in captivity, similar in the wild

Voice Deep grunts, but generally silent

Diet Wiry tufts of grass, shrubs, herbs, and lichens

Habitat Alpine tundra and steppe 13,000–19,680 ft (4,000–6,000 m); above snow line in summer

Distribution Remote areas of Tibetan plateau; Xinjiang and Qinghai (northwestern China); eastern Kashmir (India)

Status Population: probably fewer than 15,000 in the wild; IUCN Vulnerable; CITES I since 1975

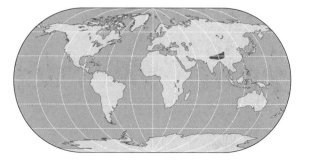

Yak

Bos grunniens

The yak is one of the highest-dwelling mammals in the world. It can survive even the harshest Himalayan winter, where its environment is a challenging combination of arctic and desert conditions.

YAK ARE AMONG THE HARDIEST mammals on earth, and their lives are a constant struggle against the elements. The adults are protected by an immensely thick, brownish-black, woolly coat. The dense underfur is covered by long, shaggy body hairs that reach almost to the ground.

Harsh Winters

Yak are fantastically hardy, surviving on the desolate high plateau of the Himalayas. Here they endure winter conditions that are among the harshest on earth, with temperatures falling to -40°F (-40°C). The high mountains are not just cold, they are also very dry, with little rain or even snowfall. Standing water is often salty, as are many of the sparse woody shrubs that the yaks eat. Yak herds wander widely in search of grasses, lichens, and other low-growing alpine plants. Their preferred food is tussocks of wiry grass, and in summer the animals may congregate in areas where the food is better than average. At high altitudes there is little to drink, and yaks consume a lot of snow in order to obtain sufficient moisture to stay alive.

    Older males are often solitary, but the yak is generally a social animal and spends most of its life as part of a herd. There are advantages to living in a group, including protection from predators like the Tibetan wolf. A group can also walk in single file through deep snow, each animal stepping in the footprints of the one in front to save energy. The leading yak picks its way with skill based on long experience. The yak's large, cloven hooves are supplemented with enlarged dewclaws, which help give better grip. Despite their huge bulk and ungainly appearance, yaks are nimble and sure-footed

climbers, able to hop from rock to rock to avoid the deepest drifts of snow. Only in the worst storms and blizzards do they come to a halt. They stand in small groups with their heads turned out of the driving wind and icy snow, waiting for better conditions to return. Being adapted to cope with extreme cold, yak are uncomfortable in warm weather. Herds that come down to the lower pastures to bear young in spring retreat rapidly as summer arrives. They return to altitudes of about 16,000 feet (5,000 m), where there is permanent snow cover. In summer the animals keep cool by wallowing in icy streams and muddy patches.

The largest herds generally include females and young, with bachelor males forming smaller bands. During the rutting season (in the fall) bulls try to gather a small herd of females for themselves. They make a distinctive grunting sound, which is the basis for the yak's scientific name. *Bos grunniens* literally means "grunting ox." The females are pregnant over winter and give birth to their calves in June. Females can only have one calf at a time and then only in alternate years, so populations grow slowly. The calves take a year to reach independence and do not breed until they are about six to eight years old. Some may live to 25 years of age.

Dying Out

Although the yak is able to survive the harshest conditions nature has to offer, it is less able to cope with threats posed by humans, including illegal hunting and competition from its domesticated relatives. Some 2,000 to 3,000 years ago the ancestors of today's yaks were successfully domesticated to provide people with milk and wool.

Today's world population of domestic yak is thought to number over 12 million. By contrast, wild yaks (which some scientists regard as a separate species, *Bos mutus*) are now extremely rare. In spite of full legal protection in all the countries where it occurs, the yak still suffers from hunting for its meat and wool. As human settlements spread, wild herds also found themselves competing with domestic animals for the sparse food on the mountains. In many cases wild yaks were simply absorbed into domestic herds; elsewhere they died out.

Domestic yak are smaller and less hardy than their wild cousins. However, the two interbreed readily, diluting the genetic purity of the wild type. They also create offspring that are less well adapted to life in the desolate conditions of the high Himalayas. Wild yak populations have been declining for many years, and there are now probably at least 20 percent fewer yak than a decade ago. It is unlikely that thousands-strong herds will ever be seen again.

⊖ *A yak lies on a rocky mountainside beneath a soaring Himalayan peak. The animal's dense, hairy coat helps conserve heat in inhospitable conditions.*

Common name Giant eland (Lord Derby's eland)

Scientific name *Taurotragus (Tragelaphus) derbianus*

Family   Bovidae

Order   Artiodactyla

Size   Length head/body: male 8–10 ft
(2.4–3.2 m); female 7–8 ft (2.1–2.4 m); tail
length: 22–31 in (55–78 cm); height at
shoulder: male 5–6 ft (1.5–1.8 m); female
4.6–5.2 ft (1.4–1.6 m)

Weight Male 990–2,000 lb
(450–907 kg); female 660–1,100
lb (300–500 kg)

Key features Large, chestnut-brown antelope with
12–15 vertical white stripes on flanks; both
sexes have long, twisted horns; raised
shoulder hump and prominent dewlap

Habits   Found in herds of up to 60 individuals but
more often 15–25; males often solitary; shy
and relatively docile creatures

Breeding   Single calf born after gestation period of 9
months. Weaned at about 4 months; females
sexually mature at 28 months, males at 18
months, but will not breed until older. May
live up to 25 years, not often kept in captivity

Voice   Deep grunts, snorts, and moos

Diet   Acacia and related trees such as *Isoberlinia*;
also other leaves, shoots, and grasses

Habitat   Woodland and forested savannas generally in
or close to *Isoberlinia* woodlands

Distribution Fragmented across northern-central Africa

Status   Population: unknown, probably under 20,000

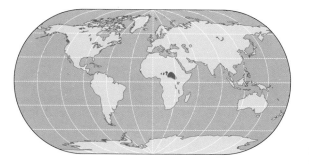

Giant Eland *Taurotragus derbianus*

*The giant eland is the largest living antelope and was
once widespread across the middle of Africa.
Nowadays it is found only in the
savanna regions of Central Africa.*

AFRICA IS HOME TO TWO SPECIES of eland—the giant
eland and the slightly smaller common eland.
Some scientists classify both in the genus
Tragelaphus. The common eland (*Taurotragus
oryx*) is widely distributed south of Uganda and
Kenya. The giant eland is found in western and
central Africa. As the largest living antelope, its
size and stature give it an oxlike appearance.

Athletic Leaps

These robust antelopes are surprisingly agile
jumpers that can leap over obstacles 6 feet
(1.8 m) high. When making a jump, they simply
walk slowly up to the obstacle, pause, lean back
slightly onto their hindquarters, and then launch
themselves into the air. It is an amazing feat for
an animal the size and stature of a cow. Giant
eland are swift creatures that can reach running
speeds of over 40 miles per hour (64 km/h).

The giant eland is sometimes split into two
separate subspecies, both of which are in
decline. The western form, *Taurotragus
derbianus derbianus*, is quite reddish in color
and bears 15 vertical white stripes on both
sides of its body. The central race, *T. d. gigas*, is
sandy colored with 12 vertical white stripes
down its body.

Both male and female giant elands carry
massive twisted horns that can reach up to 47
inches (120 cm) long in some of the males.
They are shorter and thinner in females. Males
use their horns and impressive size when
establishing dominance. The hierarchy that is
formed determines which males will have the
chance to mate. When threats are made, often
one individual will retreat, and no further
conflict will occur. However, if neither animal
retreats, horning follows, in which each

⊕ Giant eland of both sexes have long, twisted, widely splayed horns. The horns are sometimes used to break branches off trees to reach tasty leaves.

individual directs its sharp horns at its opponent's body. This may deter one of the bulls, but sometimes a challenge will be accepted, resulting in a seriously aggressive fight. Lowering their heads, they lock horns, and a struggle ensues in which each attempts to knock the other off balance. Battles for dominance will generally be settled through displays, since violent struggles can be dangerous (the strong and sharp horns of the giant eland can cause fatal injuries). Females also establish dominance hierarchies using similar rituals, but on a much smaller scale. The hierarchies that are formed appear to be based on age, size, and strength. However, giant eland are not territorial.

Giant eland are browsing animals, eating leaves nibbled from trees and shrubs. They sometimes use their horns to break branches off trees so they can reach the tasty vegetation. They prefer leguminous trees, such as acacias, and appear to be restricted to areas in and around woodlands dominated by *Isoberlinia* trees. The animals often move seasonally to exploit such trees when they come into leaf. A nomadic species, they move around at any time of the year, but especially during the dry season, when supplies of food and water are scarce. Females tend to travel farther than males. When water is available, the eland drink regularly, but they can also obtain moisture from succulents (fleshy plants) in the dry season. Their large ears are important, since the animals often feed at night and need to be alert to unseen dangers. They have an excellent sense of hearing and smell.

Ancient Paintings

Eland are one of the animals that are often depicted in the early rock art of East Africa, and today they are still important in the mythology of some southern African tribes. The meat of giant eland is of good quality, and there is plenty of it, making them a valuable target for hunters. Their milk is also high in fat and very nutritious. They are relatively docile and have been experimentally domesticated in Russia. However, the animals are accustomed to moving around a lot and may not settle well in semicaptive conditions. Giant eland have declined owing to hunting and habitat destruction, but also as a result of rinderpest, a disease to which they are highly susceptible.

Common name
Greater kudu

Scientific name
Tragelaphus strepsiceros

Family Bovidae

Order Artiodactyla

Size Length
head/body: 6–8 ft
(1.8–2.5 m); tail length: 12–22 in (30–55 cm);
height at shoulder: 39–59 in (100–150 cm)

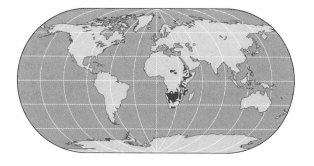

Weight Male 418–693 lb (190–314 kg); female
264–473 lb (120–214 kg)

Key features Large, slender antelope;
distinct shoulder hump; body gray- to
reddish-brown; both sides marked with
white stripes; white bands form v-shape
across muzzle; large, rounded ears; bushy tail
with white underside and black tip; mane
and crest in both sexes; long, spiral horns in
males

Habits Females and young form small herds; adult
males solitary or found in bachelor groups

Breeding Single calf born after gestation period of 7–9
months. Weaned at 6 months; females
sexually mature at about 3 years, males at 5
years. May live up to 23 years in captivity,
10–12 in the wild

Voice Barks, grunts, bleats, and whimpers; males
roar during mating season

Diet Leaves, shoots, flowers, and fruit; grass and
herbs; plants poisonous to other herbivores

Habitat Favors rocky terrain in lightly wooded areas

Distribution Widespread in southern Africa; more patchy
distribution in eastern Africa

Status Population: probably low thousands.
Declining in some areas, but generally stable

Greater Kudu

Tragelaphus strepsiceros

Male greater kudus possess distinctive and impressively long corkscrewlike horns that are sometimes used during fights to establish dominance.

THE GREATER KUDU IS ONE OF the largest and most elegant of all the antelope, standing taller than the average person. For many years the greater kudu has been hunted for sport—the male's fine spiral horns being much sought-after trophies for big-game hunters.

Height Advantage

Greater kudus are adaptable creatures that feed on a wide variety of plants. They are mainly browsers, but will graze on the lush green grass that is abundant during the rainy season. Because of their height, greater kudus can nibble at food that is out of reach of many other browsers. Although the animals often live in dry areas, they generally stay close to a water supply. They survive dry periods by storing water in their rumen (modified stomach).

As long as there are areas of cover, kudus will sometimes live near human settlements despite their nervous temperament. In such areas they are often viewed as pests because of the damage they cause to crops. But farmers cannot easily fence them out because of their astounding jumping skills: The animals can leap with ease over barriers as high as 8 feet (2.5 m).

Greater kudus are most active during the early morning and late afternoon. During the hottest part of the day they find a shady place to rest. However, in some areas they have become largely nocturnal as a result of disturbance from human activities such as hunting and farming. They are shy creatures, and when resting, they conceal themselves in woodland or thickets. Generally they are never far from cover into which they can retreat. They are also difficult to approach undetected, since their large eyes and huge mobile ears are constantly alert for danger. When moving across

⬆ An oxpecker sits on the back of a greater kudu, waiting for parasites to feed on. Female greater kudus lack the majestic horns found in the male.

open areas or approaching water to drink, they exercise great caution: Even the slightest sound may provoke them to run for cover. In woodland greater kudus are more confident, since the cover provided by their surroundings makes them less vulnerable to predators.

Loudest Antelope Call

In woodland the huge, rounded ears of the greater kudu can pick up the rustle of leaves underfoot or the breaking of a tiny branch. If the animals become frightened by a noise or sense some kind of danger, they produce a loud, harsh bark to alert others. The warning signal is possibly the loudest vocalization produced by any antelope. As they flee, they curl their tail upward so the white underside is visible, showing other kudus where to run to

escape the danger. Although they are fairly nimble, despite their large size, they are not as fast as some other species of antelope. Males have to tilt their head back when running through woodland to prevent their huge corkscrewlike horns from becoming caught on branches. Kudus are also powerful swimmers and sometimes take to water for refuge.

The distinctive spiral horns of the male are used to get at food by thrashing high branches, but their main purpose is during the rut. Rival males usually establish their status through displays, but occasionally a dispute escalates into a fight. The opponents link horns, shoving and twisting in an attempt to throw each other off balance. In extreme cases opponents' horns can lock together, and both will die—at the hands of predators or through dehydration.

Common name Common duiker (bush duiker)

Scientific name *Sylvicapra grimmia*

Family	Bovidae
Order	Artiodactyla
Size	Length head/body: male 28–41 in (70–105 cm); female 35–45 in (90–115 cm); tail length: 3–8 in (7–20 cm); height at shoulder: 18–28 in (45–70 cm)

Weight Male 24–46 lb (11–21 kg); female 26–55 lb (12–25 kg)

Key features Small antelope; face long with black band down midline to rounded, black nose; coat light gray to reddish-brown with white undersides; short, black tail with fluffy, white underside; slender, tapering horns (male only)

Habits Generally solitary; acute hearing; most active in early morning, late afternoon, and night; nocturnal in some areas due to disturbance

Breeding Usually a single lamb born after gestation period of about 7 months. Weaned at about 4–6 weeks; sexually mature at 8–9 months. May live about 14 years in captivity, 12 in the wild

Voice Alarm call is a nasal snort; bleats loudly if caught, otherwise relatively quiet

Diet Leaves, twigs, flowers, fruit, and seeds of trees and shrubs; roots and tubers; caterpillars and other insects; also frogs, lizards, small mammals, and chicks of ground-nesting birds

Habitat Prefers savannas and woodlands, but can live almost anywhere with enough food and cover; mountainous regions up to snow line

Distribution Suitable habitats across Africa south of Sahara

Status Population: abundant

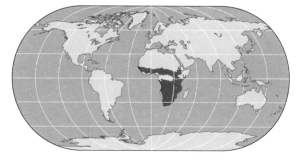

Common Duiker

Sylvicapra grimmia

The common duiker is a widespread and successful antelope species. In some African cultures duiker horn is believed to ward off evil spirits and is used to make pendants.

THERE ARE TWO BASIC TYPES OF duiker (pronounced "dike-er"). The forest duikers, of which there are about 18 species, are grouped in the genus *Cephalophus*. The common or bush duiker is a rather different creature and classified in a genus on its own (*Sylvicapra*). The common duiker differs from forest duikers in color and general shape. It has longer legs, less rounded hindquarters, and larger ears than the members of the *Cephalophus* group. Its choice of habitat is also different; the common duiker is absent from dense woodland and forest—the favored habitat of most forest duikers.

Occasional Meat-Eaters

Common duikers browse on a wide variety of trees and shrubs. Their diet includes leaves, flowers, fruit, seeds, roots, tubers, bark, and fungi. However, they are unusual among antelope because they also feed on some animal foods. They have been known to eat insects such as caterpillars, cockroaches, and ants. They will also occasionally consume lizards, frogs, small mammals, chicks of ground-nesting birds, and even dead animals. If water is available, the animals will drink, but they can survive without fluid for long periods. In fact, even if water is freely available, common duikers will not drink regularly, since they obtain much of the moisture they need from the vegetation they consume. Moisture-rich foods such as melons are especially important to common duikers living in very dry areas. It is possible that the varied diet of the common duiker is one reason why it is such a widespread and successful antelope.

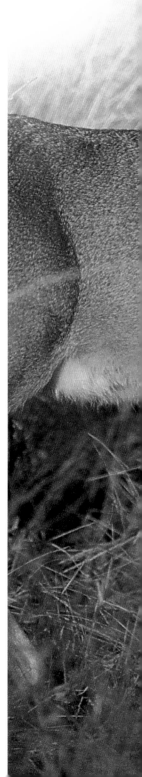

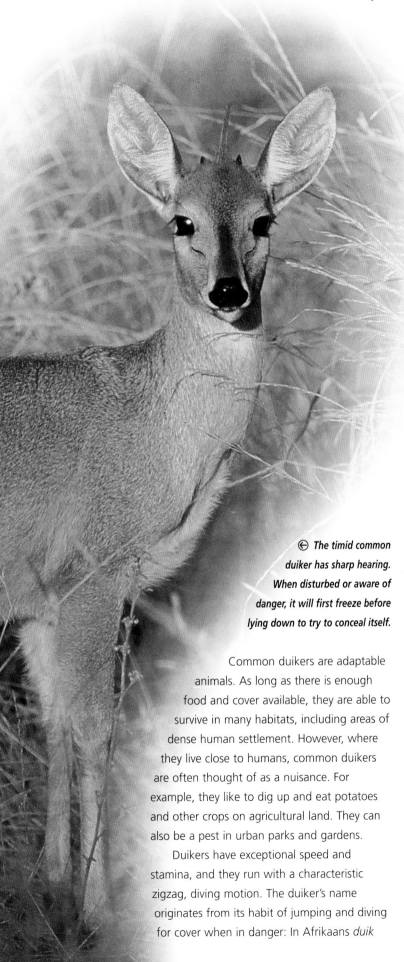

⊕ *The timid common duiker has sharp hearing. When disturbed or aware of danger, it will first freeze before lying down to try to conceal itself.*

Common duikers are adaptable animals. As long as there is enough food and cover available, they are able to survive in many habitats, including areas of dense human settlement. However, where they live close to humans, common duikers are often thought of as a nuisance. For example, they like to dig up and eat potatoes and other crops on agricultural land. They can also be a pest in urban parks and gardens.

Duikers have exceptional speed and stamina, and they run with a characteristic zigzag, diving motion. The duiker's name originates from its habit of jumping and diving for cover when in danger: In Afrikaans *duik*

means "dive." Common duikers are hunted as food by many carnivores, including eagles, leopards, cheetahs, jackals, wild dogs, and crocodiles. They are also prey for pythons. However, the sharp, pointed horns of the male duiker can be a hazard, and a python will die if its digestive system is punctured by the horns once the prey has been swallowed.

Sharply Pointed Horns

Both sexes are territorial, using scent marks to establish their terrain. Males tend to be intolerant of one another and will display to and, if necessary, fight with intruding males. Fighting involves chasing and stabbing at each other with their slender, sharply pointed horns until one of them lies down in submission or retreats. Horns are generally only found in males and may be up to 6 inches (15 cm) long. Male and female territories sometimes overlap, and a loose bond can form between two neighboring animals that are sharing part of each other's territories. The female will try to chase away any intruding females and may even butt into them to drive them off.

Common duikers pair up when breeding, and females may be seen with their young, but otherwise they are solitary animals. They rest during the hottest part of the day; but if it is cool or cloudy, they may be active almost continuously. When resting, they are solitary, females preferring to conceal themselves in low-lying and densely vegetated areas. Males tend to choose higher, more open areas, where they have clear views of their surroundings.

Common duikers are generally quiet animals. However, if caught, they will bleat loudly—a sound that attracts other duikers. If a juvenile makes the bleating alarm call, its mother will come running to help. Humans imitate the call when hunting in order to attract duikers in the area. But the antelope are resilient to heavy hunting and still widespread south of the Sahara. In fact, thanks to their adaptability, they are one of the most successful bovine species in the whole of Africa.

Common name
Blue wildebeest
(gnu)

Scientific name
Connochaetes
taurinus

Family Bovidae

Order Artiodactyla

Size Length head/body: 5.6–8 ft (1.7–2.4 m); tail
length: 24–39 in (60–100 cm); height at
shoulder: 47–59 in (120–150 cm).
Female shorter than male

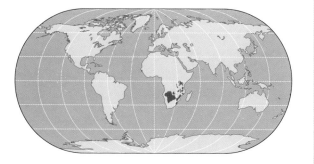

Weight Male 363–638 lb (165–290
kg); female 308–572 lb (140–260 kg)

Key features Large, cowlike antelope; humped shoulders
and deep neck; dark mane with fringe under
neck that varies in color with subspecies

Habits Gregarious: found in herds of up to 20 or 30;
herds of thousands form during migrations;
active in early morning and late afternoon

Breeding Single calf born each year after gestation
period of 8–8.5 months. Weaned at 9–12
months; females sexually mature at about 16
months, males breed later due to competition
with larger rivals. May live over 21 years in
captivity, similar in the wild

Voice Loud snorts and low moaning grunts

Diet Fresh growth of several species of grass

Habitat Savanna woodland and grassy plains

Distribution Found in 2 main areas of Africa: from Kenya
to Mozambique; also from Zambia into South
Africa

Status Population: hundreds of thousands. A
common animal

Blue Wildebeest

Connochaetes taurinus

*Wildebeest are successful animals that live at high
densities. They seek security in large numbers, since
they are important prey for many savanna carnivores.*

THE BLUE WILDEBEEST, ALSO KNOWN as the gnu, is the
common wildebeest of eastern and southern
Africa. A second species, the white-tailed gnu
(*Connochaetes gnou*), lives in South Africa and
is much less common. The wildebeest has an
odd, cowlike appearance with head, legs, and
body that almost seem to come from different
creatures. Compared with the exquisite
elegance of many other antelope found across
Africa, it appears clumsy and unattractive.
Nevertheless, the wildebeest are an extremely
significant part of the ecosystem to which they
belong. They contribute a large proportion of
the total biomass (weight of living animals) of
the savanna residents, and their grazing and
trampling habits play an important role in
shaping the landscape.

A Lion's Dinner

Wildebeest are an important prey item for
several African carnivores, in particular the lion.
For some lions at least half of their prey is made
up of that one species. The cheetah, leopard,
spotted hyena, wild dog, and crocodile are its
other main predators.

Despite their ungainly appearance, adult
wildebeest are actually quite agile animals,
possessing both speed and stamina. Yet while
being able to reach speeds of up to 50 miles
per hour (80 km/h), they can still be caught and
killed by predators, since they live mainly out on
the open grasslands where there is nowhere to
take refuge from an attack. They therefore seek
security from predators by forming large herds.
They use this "safety-in-numbers" tactic, rather
than simply trying to outrun predators.
Therefore, they do not need long legs and a
slim, streamlined body.

A blue wildebeest mudbathes in the Kalahari Gemsbok National Park, South Africa. The mud helps rid the skin and fur of irritating parasites such as lice and ticks.

The blue wildebeest's digestive system is very large. This is necessary because they are grass-eating ruminants and need a specialized system to digest their bulky food. Males also develop a heavy neck, head, and horns—important when competing for territory.

Another vital survival technique used by these creatures is the synchronization of the rut and subsequent calving period. The rut occurs during the dry season, when males dance, grunt, and bellow to attract the attention of the females, which they then herd together to mate with them. Once one male starts this activity, the others soon copy, so the whole herd's rutting behavior takes place at more or less the same time. Synchronization of the rut ensures that all the calves are born at the same time, about eight months later. Births occur during the wet season, when there is plenty of fresh green grass available for lactating mothers. Almost 90 percent of the calves are born within the space of only three weeks. Having all the young born at the same time decreases the total loss to predators. Once the predators have killed a few, they will not need more for a while. If the young were born over a longer period, the predators would be able to take far more. The birth lasts about an hour, and within only a few minutes of being born the calf is on its feet and suckling. Young wildebeest are capable of running at a very early age, vitally necessary for a large animal living out on open grassland where there is nowhere to hide.

Vital Bonds

The imprinting process, which establishes the relationship between a mother and her calf, is very important for the wildebeest, since mothers will only suckle their own young. Imprinting starts with the mother licking her young after birth and with the calf's first suckling. There are a host of dangers for the calf, so it is important that it can recognize and stay close to its mother.

Although the young stay near to their mother, they are very playful and enjoy chasing each other. If a calf becomes lost, it will bleat loudly for its mother, since without her it has little chance of survival. Hyenas, jackals, and other carnivores often try to separate a young calf from its mother so they can kill it. The mother will struggle desperately to fight off attacks from all sides. Even if the battle is eventually lost, during the time the predators have spent killing that one calf, many others will have had the opportunity to escape.

Mature females generally produce a single calf each year. It is therefore necessary for the young to fend for itself after only a year in order to make way for the new calf. With the new birth the female will not allow her calf from the previous year to continue suckling. At that point males will leave their mother and join bachelor herds, but females tend to stay in their mother's group. When the males are about four or five years old, they leave their bachelor groups to find females of their own.

Nomadic Populations

Blue wildebeest are gregarious animals, but their social structure is largely dependent on the nomadic behavior of the different populations. Movements are determined by the availability of suitable grazing and water supplies, which change seasonally. Some populations have to make extensive migrations to find fresh grass, while others enjoy year-round supplies and are relatively sedentary.

The general social organization of the blue wildebeest consists of solitary territorial males, bachelor groups, and female herds. It is the female herds that are most tightly knit. The different groups congregate in areas where there is plentiful short grass and water. Access to water is essential: Although they can last without liquid for up to five days, wildebeest normally drink every day if possible.

The bachelor groups consist of young males that have left their mothers and adult males that are not part of a mixed-sex group. They tend to be found on the edges of the area inhabited by the rest of the population. Such zones contain the least desirable areas of habitat. Female herds with their young have access to the best grazing. Where supplies are plentiful all year, the population can remain in the area. However, in places where the grass dies during the dry season, the wildebeest must follow the rains and travel to new pastures.

At certain times of year very large numbers of the animals can be seen moving together in search of food and water. The seasonal movements undertaken by many populations of wildebeest are a vital factor in their survival.

⬆ *A wildebeest mother with a newborn calf in the Masai Mara Reserve, Kenya. It is vital that the calf bonds with its mother immediately, since there are many predators looking to make a meal of a helpless baby.*

Nothing can be allowed to hold up the migration, and the wildebeest even mate on the move.

The seasonal migration of blue wildebeest across the Serengeti Plains (spanning the Kenya/Tanzania border) is an awesome sight. The animals spend the wet season, from December to April, feeding in their herds on the volcanic plains of the eastern branch of the Great Rift Valley. Once the rains stop and the grasses dry out, they must move on. If they stayed, they would face starvation. The herds are so vast that from the air the migration looks like a black river snaking across the plains. The animals move eastward toward the grasslands of Lake Victoria. As the dry season takes hold, the herds travel north to the woodland areas of the Masai Mara. Their progress is slow and sporadic: On average they cover not much more than 5 or 6 miles (8 or 9 km) each day. The annual movements allow the grasses to replenish themselves before the wildebeest return. By avoiding overexploitation

of the food sources, migrating wildebeest can build up much higher populations than the purely sedentary herds.

Success Story

Wildebeest are very successful animals that have evolved to live at high densities on an unstable food source. However, in the 1880s the animals became threatened by a cattle disease known as rinderpest. The disease reached Africa by accident, brought from India by European settlers. Fortunately, a cattle vaccination plan carried out in the 1950s and 1960s gave the wildebeest a chance to recover, and today they are thriving once again. In the Serengeti and Masai Mara wildebeest now make up 60 percent of the total large mammal population. However, space is very important for these savanna-dwelling animals. Increasingly, large areas of grassland are being fenced off to keep cattle and other livestock. Artificial barriers interfere with the traditional migration of the wildebeest and threaten its success.

Enough for Everyone

The blue wildebeest can be found on the Serengeti, where it co-exists with several other hoofed herbivores. The animals are able to live together because they share the food. Blue wildebeest, zebra, and topi all feed on the same species of grasses. However, they each feed on the grass at a different stage of growth. Zebra and topi eat the old grass, but blue wildebeest concentrate on the young shoots. Other herbivores feed in the same places, but eat different species of grasses—often after the zebras and wildebeest have cleared the longer growth and made new grasses accessible to the smaller species. The savannas are therefore able to support a far greater quantity and variety of wild animals than if domestic cattle lived there instead, since they all eat the same things.

⊕ *Wildebeest cross a river on their annual migration to fresh feeding grounds. It can be a risky process, since the animals may drown or fall victim to waiting crocodiles.*

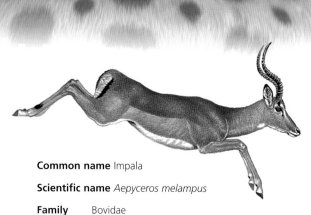

Common name Impala

Scientific name *Aepyceros melampus*

Family   Bovidae

Order   Artiodactyla

Size   Length head/body: 47–63 in (120–160 cm); tail length: 12–18 in (30–45 cm); height at shoulder: 30–37 in (75–95 cm)

      Weight Male 99–176 lb (45–80 kg); female 88–132 lb (40–60 kg)

Key features Medium-sized, sleek, and lightly built antelope; long, slender legs; characteristic tuft of black hair on lower and rear edge of hind legs; upper body bright reddish-brown, sides fawn, and underparts white; black-tipped ears, white eyebrows; male bears slender, ridged horns

Habits   Gregarious; acute senses: explosion of activity when disturbed; social structure differs with season; mostly active during day, although avoids midday sun; some nocturnal activity

Breeding   Generally single calf born each year after gestation period of 6.5 months. Weaned at 5–7 months; females sexually mature at 18 months, males at 12–13 months. May live about 15 years in captivity, similar in the wild

Voice   High-pitched bark and snorts when alarmed; males roar, snort, and growl during rut

Diet   Grass; also leaves and shoots; fruit and seeds of trees and bushes

Habitat   Open woodlands and grasslands

Distribution Central and southeastern Africa from Kenya to South Africa; small population in southwestern Africa around southern Angola

Status   Population: many thousands; IUCN Least Concern; one subspecies listed as Vulnerable; may be declining in parts of its range

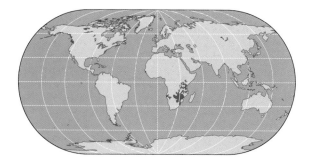

Impala

Aepyceros melampus

With a lightly built frame and long, slender legs, the impala is an elegant antelope that is famous for its agility, grace, and beauty.

WHILE SOME SPECIES OF ANTELOPE prefer to live in open grasslands and others in deep forest, the impala is typically found in open woodland and areas where the trees blend into grassland.

Inhabitant of "Ecotones"

During the wet season, when the plains are green with the fresh growth brought on by the rains, impala can be found grazing on the new, lush grasses. When the rains end, the grasses dry out, and the adaptable antelope move toward woodland areas. There they find nourishment from the leaves, shoots, fruit, and seeds of trees and bushes. Consequently, impala prefer to inhabit so-called "ecotones," the transition zones between open grasslands and woodlands, where they can use the varying food resources available with the seasons. Being able to switch their feeding habits means that impala need not undertake lengthy migrations. However, because they need a highly specific habitat (including cover, moisture, and year-round nourishment), the animals will either be found in large numbers or not at all.

Impala are adapted to living at high densities, making them a frequent target of many of the larger predators, including lions, cheetahs, leopards, wild dogs, and hyenas. However, the sprightly antelope can be a difficult meal to catch. The benefit of living in large groups is that there are always numerous eyes and ears on the lookout for danger. If an impala becomes aware of danger, it barks an alarm call to the rest of the herd. As the predator moves closer, more alarm calls are sounded; if it attempts to attack, impalas take flight in an explosion of activity. The lightly built antelope are extremely fleet of foot. They leap

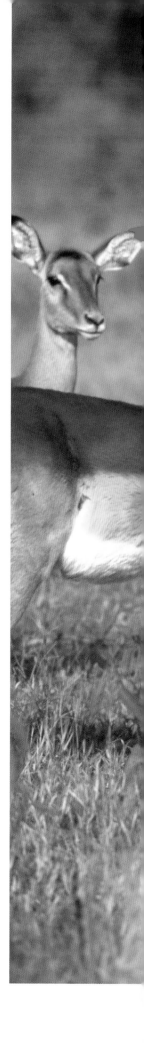

Social Organization

Impala organize themselves into bachelor, breeding, and nursery herds. Bachelor herds include adult males that are potential territory holders and juvenile males. Breeding herds contain adult and juvenile females, juvenile males, and at times other than the rut, a number of adult males. Sometimes nursery herds of juveniles occur, but they are only temporary groups that will later disperse and become part of the breeding herds. In some areas males are territorial throughout the year, but in southern parts males establish their territory just for the period of the rut. They will defend their territory aggressively, using vocalizations and displays including head-bobbing, horn-clashing, and head-pushing. Bouts of serious fighting may occur. The horns are vital weapons and indicators of status, used for head-to-head wrestling. Only present in males, they are distinctive structures that sweep upward, out, and backward in a lyre shape. The sharp horns can cause serious injuries or even death. They may grow up to 31 inches (80 cm) long, but the average is about 20 inches (50 cm).

The impala is an important member of its ecosystem. Its grazing habits help shape the landscape, and it is a valuable prey item for many predators. There is also an important relationship between impala, termites, and acacia trees. During the dry season when grass is scarce, impala feed on the ripe pods of the acacia. The seeds pass through the gut unharmed and are dispersed in the impala's droppings. Termites also use the acacia as a source of food, and in some areas the dead thorn trees are an important part of their diet. Star grass, attractive nourishment for impalas, often grows on the side of deserted termite mounds. While feeding on it, the impala nourishes the soil with its droppings.

wildly in all directions, confusing the predator as they vanish into nearby bushes. Impressive athletes, they make astounding jumps that carry them over distances of up to 40 feet (12 m). With apparently little effort they appear to float gracefully through the air, clearing obstacles up to 8 feet (2.5 m) high. Speeding into dense vegetation, the impala can also weave through narrow gaps in the trees without hesitation. When fleeing from danger, it kicks out its hind feet, releasing scent from the black tufted ankle glands. The scent trail helps the individuals regroup after the chase, especially if they have fled into dense cover.

⬆ A group of impala in Lake Nakuru National Park, Kenya. Impala live in highly specific habitats with year-round nourishment and therefore do not need to undertake migrations.

Common name Topi

Scientific name *Damaliscus lunatus*

Family	Bovidae
Order	Artiodactyla

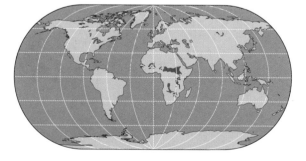

Size Length head/body: 5–7.5 ft (1.5–2.3 m); tail length: 16–24 in (40–60 cm); height at shoulder: 39–51 in (100–130 cm)

Weight Male 264–352 lb (120–160 kg); female 165–231 lb (75–105 kg)

Key features Largish antelope with long, narrow face, short neck, and high shoulders; glossy reddish-brown coat with upperpart of legs darker (often blue-gray); dark blaze on face; tail ends with black tassel; both sexes carry ringed horns

Habits Social: small herds with larger aggregations occurring on favored feeding grounds; groups of territorial males, breeding, and bachelor herds also form; generally inquisitive animals

Breeding Single calf born after gestation period of 7.5–8 months. Weaned at 6 months; females sexually mature at about 1.5 years, males at 3 years. May live up to about 15 years in captivity, similar in the wild

Voice Snorts and grunts

Diet Almost exclusively grazers with a preference for grass up to 20 in (50 cm) tall

Habitat Savannas and floodplains

Distribution Various subspecies found in suitable habitats throughout sub-Saharan Africa

Status Population: about 300,000; IUCN Least Concern. Local populations and some subspecies threatened by habitat destruction

Topi

Damaliscus lunatus

The topi has distinctive patches of gray on a brown body, a long face, and robust horns. A notable feature of the species is that the males and females look alike.

AFRICA IS HOME TO SEVERAL SEPARATE subspecies of topi that vary in size, color, and horn development. The korrigum (*D. l. korrigum*) is the largest of the subspecies. It has well-developed horns and can be found in West Africa. The smaller tiang (*D. l. tiang*) has more slender horns, is redder in color, and lives in East Africa. The tsessebe (*D. l. lunatus*), which is a dark-chestnut color, occurs in southern Africa, and the typical topi (*D. l. jimela* and *D. l. topi*) occur in East Africa and the Democratic Republic of Congo.

On Guard

Topi are sizable antelope that would make a satisfying meal for any large predator. However, the number of adult topi that fall prey to such carnivores is relatively small, since they are fast and extremely alert animals. Topi are well known for their use of termite mounds as lookout posts. A "sentry" will use such a vantage point to survey the surrounding area, sometimes standing for hours watching for danger or unwelcome intruders.

The topi's ability to reach speeds in excess of 45 miles per hour (70 km/h), along with its wary behavior, often means it can escape being the next meal of a hungry lion. Unfortunately, its vigilance cannot save it from the hunter's gun, and its inquisitive nature also contributes to its vulnerability; it has been known to stay out in the open even when a hunter has shot fellow members of the herd. In addition, although adults can often escape the clutches of a predator, the young calves are extremely susceptible to attacks from both large and small carnivores. Synchronization of births helps reduce the loss of newborn calves, but the growing youngsters are still at risk.

⊕ A topi stands sentry on a mound in Kenya's Masai Mara game reserve. Topi are very alert animals that often use of termite mounds as lookout posts.

As grazers, topi can often be found mixing with herds of wildebeest, zebra, and other herbivores. Topi like to eat long grass, leaving it trimmed short and allowing access for other species that prefer shorter forage. But old, long grass is often tough and contains abrasive silica. It can also be contaminated with dust or earth spattered by rains. Feeding on the gritty food, the topi's teeth get worn down fairly fast. Older animals lose their ability to chew food properly, and worn teeth may even fall out.

Variable Behavior

The grazers of the African plains are bound together by their need for grass and may even share migration routes. However, not all topi undertake seasonal movements, producing variable social behavior among different populations. The males of sedentary topi herds have a harem of females that stay with them and help defend the territory. Topi are unusual among antelope in that males and females look alike. It is even possible for females to fool intruders into believing them to be males by performing displays and posturing. Males that belong to migratory populations of topi cannot keep a permanent or large territory. Instead, they own small, temporary territories that they use during the rut to gather breeding females.

Several species of antelope hide their young to protect them from predators, the mothers returning to feed their calves when necessary. However, newborn topi tend to stay with the breeding herd, where they receive both concealment and protection. As the mothers feed, the young join together in little nursery groups with one or more females close by. The rest of the breeding herd will return to protect the young if alerted to signs of danger. Females care for their young for about a year, after which they produce their next calf. The females are fertile throughout their lives, even when they are losing their last teeth.

Topi need grass, water, and shelter, and are often found on the edges of grassland close to wooded areas. However, rather than hiding in the woodland, they tend to use trees to shelter from the scorching African sun. During the dry season topi are often found on floodplains following the dwindling water supplies. They need to drink regularly when feeding on dry grasses, but are not so dependent on water during the rainy season when the grasses are juicy. When the rains arrive, the antelope have to move away from the floodplains to higher ground. They take the opportunity to feed on the succulent grasses that flourish as the land is refreshed by the long-awaited rains.

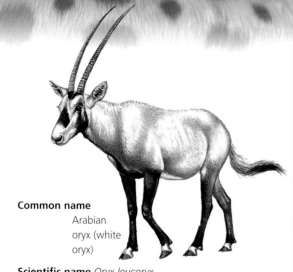

Common name
Arabian oryx (white oryx)

Scientific name *Oryx leucoryx*

Family Bovidae

Order Artiodactyla

Size Length head/body: 5–5.2 ft (1.5–1.6 m); tail length: about 16–20 in (40–50 cm); height at shoulder: 31–39 in (80–100 cm)

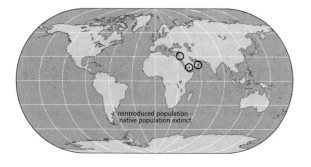

Weight 140–155 lb (64–70 kg)

Key features Slender white antelope with straight horns (in both sexes); legs black, each with white band above hoof; face has dark markings

Habits Lives in small herds, wandering widely in search of sparse food

Breeding Single calf born at any time of year after gestation period of 240 days. Weaned at 4.5 months; sexually mature at about 3 years, but males unlikely to breed until older. May live up to 20 years in captivity, usually fewer in the wild

Voice Normally silent

Diet Grasses and desert shrubs

Habitat Dry, stony deserts

Distribution Formerly in Egypt, Iraq, Israel, Syria, United Arab Emirates, and Yemen. Now reintroduced to Jordan, Oman, and Saudi Arabia

Status Population: about 1,000 in the wild, plus 6,500 in captivity; IUCN Endangered (wild populations formerly extinct, but reintroduced to Jordan, Oman, and Saudi Arabia); CITES I

reintroduced population –
native population extinct

Arabian Oryx

Oryx leucoryx

The Arabian oryx is the whitest species of oryx, superbly adapted to life in the desert. It was hunted to extinction in the wild, and has been reintroduced to parts of its former range, but is now threatened again.

ARABIAN ORYX ARE TRUE DESERT animals, but they favor stony plains over soft sand or rocky mountain slopes. The harsh conditions cause the vegetation to be sparse, except in some coastal regions where fog and dew encourage lusher growth. Little rain falls in the dry, stony desert—sometimes none at all.

Conserving Supplies

Oryx avoid eating too much from the same place by living only in small herds of usually fewer than 10 animals. The animals also move around, traveling from one feeding place to another over a vast area. They generally eat in the early part of the day, rest, then feed again before finding shade for the hottest period in the afternoon. They seem able to detect rain at a distance and travel to the area affected, benefiting from the new growth of plants. They move around seasonally between good feeding places, roaming an area of several hundred square miles in a year.

The Arabian oryx was formerly widespread in the deserts of the Middle East. It was hunted by local people for sport and meat; but as long as the hunts were on foot or used camels for transport, the animal could usually escape into the vast, inhospitable deserts. Despite their ability to flee, oryx were progressively eliminated from countries such as Syria, Egypt, and Israel, where they had once been present. By the 1950s use of four-wheel-drive vehicles, abundant fuel, automatic rifles, and oil-based local wealth combined to make hunting in Arab countries more frequent and more successful. As a result, the Arabian oryx was hunted to extinction in the wild. The last free-living individuals probably died in the early 1970s.

Pioneering Project

By that time several countries had already kept and bred the oryx in captivity, and international cooperation between zoos brought together a few animals in Phoenix, Arizona, in 1963. There the climate is similar to the original home of the oryx, and the animals bred well. From the beginning the aim was not to exhibit yet another species in a zoo, but to breed enough animals to allow them to be reintroduced to the wild. It was the first such international project for any threatened species, and many other animals are now treated in a similar way.

Arabian oryx were released in Oman in 1982, Jordan in 1983, and Saudi Arabia in 1990. There are now over 1,000 individuals living wild in the three areas, plus many more in zoos such as Los Angeles. However, the project is not without its difficulties. Released animals do not know how to migrate seasonally to take advantage of the dispersed rainfall. As a result, they have to be supplied with food and water until they learn how to use their new environment. In addition, captive-bred populations are vulnerable to natural disasters such as disease and drought. Since oryx produce only one calf at a time, they cannot rapidly make good any losses.

More seriously, a renewed period of hunting threatens the success of the project— this time to catch live animals for sale to private zoos and animal collectors. Since 1996 the Oman population has been reduced from about 400 animals to 50, al of which are male. Apart from reducing numbers, the effects of the high-speed chases disrupt the herds, causing females to lose their young, and probably resulting in deaths from heat stress. Many oryx have now been taken back into captivity to begin breeding again. The aim is to ensure the success of the population when the threat from poachers has been overcome.

The oryx's white coat has evolved to reflect solar radiation. The horns, present in both males and females, were once valued as trophies by big-game hunters.

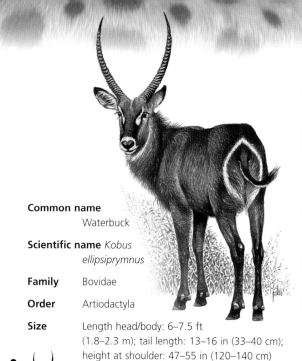

Common name
Waterbuck

Scientific name *Kobus ellipsiprymnus*

Family Bovidae

Order Artiodactyla

Size Length head/body: 6–7.5 ft (1.8–2.3 m); tail length: 13–16 in (33–40 cm); height at shoulder: 47–55 in (120–140 cm)

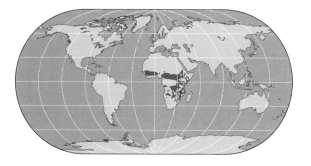

Weight Male 440–660 lb (200–300 kg); female 352–440 lb (160–200 kg)

Key features Robust antelope; coat long, coarse, and gray-brown to reddish; face dark with white chin; pale bands above eyes; shortish tail with dark tuft; broad white ring around rump; rounded ears; heavily ridged horns in males

Habits Social: herds usually 6–12 in number, occasionally larger; adult males solitary and territorial; always lives close to water

Breeding Single calf born each year after gestation period of 8.5–9 months. Weaned at 6–9 months; females sexually mature at 18 months, males at 3 years but both breed later. May live about 18 years in captivity, similar in the wild

Voice Mothers bleat or snort when calling young

Diet Grasses, water plants, leaves, and shoots

Habitat Savanna, flood plains, woodland, and scrub; must be close to permanent source of water

Distribution Most of Africa south of Sahara as far south as northeastern South Africa

Status Population: 200,000; IUCN Least Concern. Declining

Waterbuck

Kobus ellipsiprymnus

Waterbuck are water-dependent antelope, never far from a reliable source of water. Their name, however, may be misleading, since although they are good swimmers, they spend most of their time on dry land.

WATERBUCK ARE ALWAYS FOUND close to water, since they need to drink regularly to keep their bodies cool. During hot weather most antelope and gazelles are able to concentrate their urine to avoid water loss. However, waterbuck—and also the lechwe (*Kobus leche*), a closely related species—are not capable of saving water in this manner. Instead, they must drink often to avoid dehydration in the hot African climate.

Hidden Danger

Waterbuck are not really at home in water and in that way are typical antelope of the African savanna. However, they are good swimmers and will enter deep water to escape terrestrial predators. Unfortunately, they are not always secure in water, since it is the hunting ground of another fearsome carnivore—the crocodile—in whose diet they often feature.

The waterbuck's coat hairs are covered in a smelly, greasy secretion that is thought to be a method of waterproofing. Its characteristic shaggy coat probably adds to its already high water requirements, since the animal is unable to withstand any amount of heat exposure without needing to drink to cool itself down. Although the animal is somewhat limited in its choice of habitat, the vegetation near permanent water sources is generally plentiful. It can also feed on water plants during the dry season, when grass is limited.

In Africa there are two subspecies of waterbuck, *Kobus e. ellipsiprymnus* and *K. e. defassa*. They are similar in build and form, only really differing in color, markings, and distribution. The common waterbuck is found in southern and eastern Africa. It is usually gray-brown in color, and the rump bears a broad

⬅ The waterbuck's long-haired coat looks shaggy in comparison with the sleek coats of other African antelope. The horns in the male sweep upward in an arc.

white ring. The defassa waterbuck, on the other hand, is distributed across northeastern, central, and western Africa. It has a more reddish tinge to its coat and wide white patches on the rump.

The social organization of the waterbuck is influenced by its rather sedentary lifestyle. The animals do not migrate, so adult males are territorial all year round. Although males become sexually mature by the age of three years, they do not generally establish a territory before they are six years old. Young males and nonterritorial adults can be found in bachelor herds, where they remain until they gain sufficient dominance to take a territory.

Ferocious Fights

Waterbuck males bear a handsome but lethal pair of sharply pointed horns. They are used as defensive weapons against predators (territorial bulls will sometimes even confront lions) and during fights with rival males. Displays will occasionally chase off a rival, but serious fights are quite common in waterbuck. The skin on the neck of males is thick, providing protection during a fight, but the ferocity of the struggles can lead to fatalities. Territorial males will sometimes allow other mature bulls to attach themselves to their territory. The "satellite" males help the territorial male defend his terrain. In return they get the protection of a territory, the opportunity to mate when the territorial male is absent, and possibly the chance of acquiring the territory later on.

Wet-Season Socializing

Female herds tend to consist of six to 12 individuals, but sometimes aggregations of 30 or more may form. Females have large overlapping home ranges and are constantly passing through male territories. In general, waterbuck aggregate in the wet season when food is plentiful. They spread out more during the dry season when food becomes scarce. Ultimately, the size of herds and territories depends on the resources available; but if densities become high and the habitat begins to deteriorate, some animals will move on.

The distinctive musky, goatlike smell of the waterbuck is so strong that it can sometimes be recognized from a distance by the human nose. The smell, along with the discovery of only partly eaten carcasses, suggests that predators may not favor the meat. However, a significantly high number of waterbuck are killed by predators, perhaps because they are easy to catch. Fortunately, waterbuck are generally safe from human hunters, since most people dislike the musky-tasting flesh.

Common name Thomson's gazelle (tommy)

Scientific name *Eudorcas thomsoni*

Family	Bovidae
Order	Artiodactyla
Size	Length head/body: 31–47 in (80–120 cm); tail length: 6–11 in (15–27 cm); height at shoulder: 22–32 in (55–82 cm)
	Weight Male 44–77 lb (20–35 kg); female 33–55 lb (15–25 kg)
Key features	Small, slender antelope; pale-brown coat, white underside; bold black band from shoulder to flank; white ring around eyes and boldly striped face; ridged, parallel horns curve backward with tips turning forward; female horns shorter and thinner than male's
Habits	Migratory; lives in herds of 60 or more, led by a single female; mature males not associated with a harem are often solitary and territorial
Breeding	Generally single offspring born up to twice a year after gestation period of 5–6 months. Weaned at 4–5 months; females sexually mature at about 9 months, males first breed at about 3 years. May live about 16 years in captivity, 10 in the wild
Voice	Feeble bleats and whistles
Diet	Fresh green grass in rains; herbs, foliage, and seeds of shrubs in dry season
Habitat	Open savanna grasslands
Distribution	Suitable habitats in Tanzania and Kenya; also isolated population in southern Sudan
Status	Population: probably around 500,000; IUCN Near Threatened

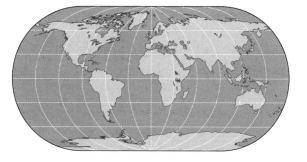

Thomson's Gazelle

Eudorcas thomsoni

The boldly striped Thomson's gazelle has a constantly flicking black tail that seems to portray an air of nervous activity—even in the heat of the midday sun.

THOMSON'S GAZELLE IS ONE OF the few mammals that characteristically lives right out in the open on the short grasses of the African plains, rarely if ever seeking cover among shrubs. The open plains, with grass barely 1 inch (2.5 cm) high, offer no cover and make the gazelles highly conspicuous to predators. Lions, cheetahs, leopards, and wild dogs prey on them, and their young are also hunted by jackals, hyenas, baboons, pythons, and eagles.

Stalking the Predator

Thomson's gazelles, or "tommies" as they are often called, have an acute sense of sight and smell, as well as excellent hearing. If a member of the herd spots a predator, it will snort an alarm call; and with their tails constantly flicking, the gazelles group together and move toward the danger. As they get closer to the predator, the numbers in the apparently foolhardy group increase. With all eyes staring intently at the source of danger, they approach until they are surprisingly near the enemy.

Leaving themselves at a crucially safe flight distance, the gazelles follow the hunter. Although their behavior may seem slightly strange, by stalking their stalker, they are drawing attention to it and so destroying any chance of a surprise ambush. If they are attacked, the herd will dash off, leaping from side to side and creating a highly confusing target for the predator to pursue.

Living in large herds therefore provides the gazelles with a certain degree of protection. With so many pairs of ears and eyes on the alert, predators find it hard to approach the herd unnoticed. Large numbers can confuse the

A mother and calf. Mothers hide their newborn calves, returning several times a day to feed them. The infant's tawny coat helps it remain undetected.

hunters. With more choice for the predator, the odds of any one individual falling victim are reduced, especially if the predator is distracted into changing its mind about which animal to chase. The vulnerability of tommies on the open plains is therefore balanced by the vigilant behavior of the herds and the safety in numbers that they provide.

About 15 races of Thomson's gazelle have been described based on variation in color and horn size. They prefer to graze on short grasses and are often found feeding with larger herbivores, including wildebeest and zebra. These bigger animals trample and crop the tall grasses, allowing the gazelles access to short-grass turf. Interactions of this kind between equids and similarly sized ruminant grazers are not uncommon.

If they can obtain moisture from their food, Thomson's gazelles are able to go without drinking water for a while; but if the grass is dry, they will need to drink daily. Tommies often congregate on grasslands that have been burned, since they favor the tiny new green shoots that sprout after a fire. In the dry season they incorporate herbs, foliage, and seeds into their diet to make up for the lack of fresh grass. Like many other grazers, they migrate annually according to the season, searching for new pastures to provide them with the nourishment they require.

Playful Young

Thomson's gazelles breed twice a year. Although calves can be born at any time in the annual cycle, there tends to be a distinct peak toward the end of the rainy seasons when food is plentiful. When the calves are strong enough, they will join the rest of the herd. The young calves in the herd are extremely playful; and when the herds come together in the early morning and late afternoon, they can be seen jumping in the air and sprinting together.

Breeding males are highly territorial. They mark their land and defend it vigorously. The forceful battles that result sometimes end in serious injury as the combatants lock horns and struggle for ownership. It is a vitally important contest, since without territory of their own males would probably not get the opportunity to mate. Successful males will try to mate with any receptive female that enters their territory, and to herd breeding females onto their land.

Although their numbers have declined recently due to habitat loss, competition with livestock, and the activities of meat poachers, tommies are still the most common gazelles in East Africa and not threatened at present.

Common name
Springbok

Scientific name *Antidorcas marsupialis*

Family Bovidae

Order Artiodactyla

Size Length head/body: 47–59 in (120–150 cm); tail length: 6–11 in (14–28 cm); height at shoulder: 27–35 in (68–90 cm)

Weight Male 66–130 lb (30–59 kg); female 44–95 lb (20–43 kg)

Key features Slender antelope; dark reddish-brown band separates cinnamon-brown upperparts from white underparts; fold of skin extends from back to rump, showing crest of white hair when opened; face white with reddish-brown stripe; long, narrow ears; short, ridged horns

Habits Gregarious: up to 1,500 individuals may move to fresh pastures during wet season; smaller herds in dry season

Breeding Usually single offspring born after gestation period of 6 months. Weaned at 4 months; females sexually mature at 7 months, males at about 12 months. May live up to 19 years in captivity, 10 in the wild

Voice Loud grunting bellows, high-pitched whistling snorts, bleats, and low-pitched bellows

Diet Fresh new grass; leaves and flowers of shrubs and trees; also digs for roots and bulbs

Habitat Prefers open habitats, arid plains, savanna, and semidesert habitats

Distribution Southern Angola, Namibia, Botswana, and South Africa

Status Population: 2–2.5 million; IUCN Least Concern

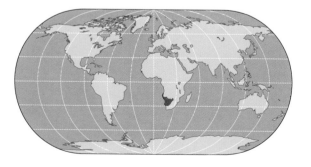

Springbok

Antidorcas marsupialis

The colorful springbok—so called because of its characteristic stiff-legged jumping behavior—is a highly distinctive antelope that is both a national and sporting icon of South Africa.

AT THE BEGINNING OF THE 20TH century visitors to southern Africa could have witnessed the astounding migrations of springbok following the rains in search of fresh pastures.

Mass Migration

The treks of the enormous herds, sometimes containing hundreds of thousands of animals, covered vast expanses of land. Some of the migrating masses were so numerous that it would take days for the whole herd to pass a given point. An estimate of the size of one such trek stated that it covered land over 100 miles (160 km) long and 15 miles (24 km) wide. It is thought that such mass movements were initiated by periods of drought and rainfall within the springboks' range. The herds would move to areas where rains had stimulated the growth of lush vegetation. The remarkable migrations also illustrate the springbok's geographical awareness—individuals were able to return "home" to a small territory after undertaking the extensive journeys.

Moving in such large numbers, springbok caused a fair amount of damage to the land over which they traveled. The treks also led to the death of many animals as a result of starvation, disease, predation, and drowning. The development of farms and human settlements following colonization by Europeans led to a huge reduction in springbok numbers. Fences created artificial barriers on the migration routes, and large populations could not be sustained when they were prevented from migrating. Unable to follow the rains to fresh pastures, there was not enough food for them all. In addition, hunting pressures from

↑ Two springbok males fighting. Hunting contributed to a fall in springbok numbers in the 19th and 20th centuries. Today the animal is the national emblem of South Africa.

succulent vegetation. They also scrape away the soil, seeking roots and bulbs, and sometimes feed on fruit with a high water content. Where water is available, they will drink even if it is very salty. But they can survive indefinitely without drinking if they can find food that contains enough moisture.

farmers, whose crops were being destroyed by the treks, led to further losses. Today the movements of springbok can still be observed, but on a much smaller scale and only in unfenced areas.

Heat Reflection

Springbok tend to be most active in the early morning and late afternoon, but their routine can vary according to the weather. When feeding, they position themselves with their white rumps toward the sun. White reflects the radiation of the sun's scorching rays, preventing the animal from becoming too hot. In the same way the white color of their underside reflects heat from the ground. They also have a thin coat, an adaptation that aids heat loss. It is especially useful during periods of activity—for example, when fleeing a predator. Springbok occur in arid areas where there is little or no surface water available, but the animals are able to obtain the moisture they need from

Stotting and Pronking

The habit of repeatedly leaping into the air, with all four legs held stiffly downward, is seen when the animals are startled, being chased, or even in play. It is known as stotting or pronking. Springing from the ground to heights of 6.5 to 10 feet (2 to 3 m), the animals hold their legs stiff and their body arched. When they descend, all four legs land simultaneously, and then the animals shoot back into the air with no apparent effort. It looks as though the legs contain springs, which in effect they do. The force of landing is absorbed by stretching muscles and tendons, which then act like elastic and catapult the animal back into the air. Stotting is also seen occasionally in other related species such as impala and Thomson's gazelle. While stotting, the springbok displays the crest of white hair on the back that is normally hidden in a pouchlike fold of skin (the origin of their scientific name, _marsupialis_). Stotting is possibly used by the animals to locate the position of predators and to communicate with other members of the herd.

Common name
Gerenuk
(giraffe-
gazelle)

Scientific name *Litocranius walleri*

Family Bovidae

Order Artiodactyla

Size Length head/body: 4.6–5.2 ft (1.4–1.6 m); tail length: 10–14 in (25–35 cm); height at shoulder: 31–41 in (80–105 cm)

Weight Male 68–114 lb (31–52 kg); female 62–99 lb (28–45 kg)

Key features Slender antelope with exceptionally long neck; long, thin legs; narrow, elongated muzzle; coat reddish-brown, flanks a lighter buff; inside of ears patterned black and white; tail ends with black tuft; males have large, ringed horns that hook forward at tip

Habits Social organization includes solitary territorial males, groups of adult females and their young, and small groups of bachelor males

Breeding Single offspring born after gestation period of 6.5–7 months. Weaned at about 4–6 months; females sexually mature at about 1 year, males at 1.5 years. May live 10–12 years in the wild; rarely kept in captivity

Voice Humming grunts, low rumbles, and a buzzing sound when alarmed; whistles and bleats

Diet Leaves, fruit, flowers, buds, and twigs of trees and shrubs; direct water supply unnecessary

Habitat Dry areas with brush and thorn scrub

Distribution Arid areas of East Africa, including parts of Ethiopia, Somalia, Kenya, and Tanzania

Status Population: 95,000; IUCN Near Threatened

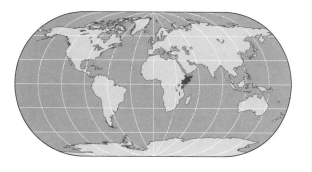

Gerenuk

Litocranius walleri

With its characteristic long, slender neck and tiny face, the rather strange-looking gerenuk is one of the easiest antelope to identify.

NOT SURPRISINGLY, THE GERENUK is named after its distinctive long neck: The Somali word *gerenuk* means "giraffe-necked." It is also sometimes called the giraffe-gazelle. The gerenuk is a strict browser that feeds on the leaves, shoots, and fruit of several different trees and shrubs.

Stretching for Food

Gerenuks have a special technique that allows them to use food not reached by other antelope. Rising on their hind legs and stretching out the long neck, they can browse on foliage at heights of over 6.5 feet (2 m), well beyond the reach of other species. Giraffes are their only competitors. A gerenuk can also use its forelimbs to pull higher branches down within reach. Its small, neat muzzle allows it to reach leaves from among thorny tangles that deter other browsers. Fitting into such a specific feeding niche permits the gerenuk to live alongside many other herbivores without competing with them for food.

Independent from Water

The nutritious mix of succulent leaves, buds, flowers, and fruit on which the gerenuk feeds provides the animal with all the moisture it needs, as well as sustenance. In fact, the species has managed to gain independence from normal water supplies. Gerenuks that live near water may drink occasionally; but if water is not available, they need not drink at all.

Predators of the gerenuk include lions, cheetahs, leopards, and wild dogs. Gerenuks are wary and shy creatures. If an animal becomes suspicious, it will hide behind a bush, stand motionless, and peer around the cover with its long neck to investigate. If startled or alerted to danger, possibly by the loud bleat of

another gerenuk, it will run away. Gerenuks are not particularly swift in comparison with other antelope. Their long neck—so useful at other times—can be a cumbersome problem during running. In dense thorn scrub they move with a stealthy, crouched trot, with the neck and tail held out horizontally.

No Need to Roam

Because of their specialized feeding habits, gerenuks can be resident in the same area throughout the year. They do not need to undertake long migrations in search of fresh grass and water as so many other African antelope do. However, gerenuks have large home ranges within which they make small seasonal movements in search of food.

Males begin to stake out a territory when they are about three years old. They defend their own space from other adult males, but will tolerate and often associate with female groups that pass through. The total range area is so large that each individual concentrates only on the core, using scent, droppings, and urine to signal ownership.

Female groups with their young move over ranges of about 1 to 2 square miles (2.5 to 5 sq. km), traveling freely in and out of male territories. The ranges of such female groups frequently overlap, and the animals sometimes form larger, temporary aggregations. Young males that leave their mothers but are too young to take a territory of their own sometimes join with other such males. They move from place to place trying to avoid confrontations with territorial males.

The unusual but attractive gerenuk was eliminated from some areas of Africa by hunters who slaughtered it for skins. It is still relatively widespread in the drier parts of eastern Africa, but much of the population is outside protected areas and numbers are declining.

⊕ *The gerenuk is able to stand almost vertically on its hind legs. It holds branches with its forelegs and plucks succulent leaves using the long tongue and upper lip.*

Common name American bighorn sheep

Scientific name *Ovis canadensis*

Family	Bovidae
Order	Artiodactyla
Size	Length head/body: male 5.5–6.2 ft (1.7–1.9 m); female 4.9–5.2 ft (1.5–1.6 m); tail length: 3–5 in (7–12 cm); height at shoulder: 27.5–43 in (70–110 cm)
	Weight Male 126–310 lb (57–140 kg); female 125–175 lb (57–80 kg)
Key features	Brown body; white muzzle, underparts, and rump patch; brown horns—large and curled in rams, smaller and straighter in ewes
Habits	Active by day; sociable: congregates in same-sex groups of 5–15 animals
Breeding	Usually single lamb born after gestation period of about 175 days. Weaned around 4–5 months; females sexually mature at 4–5 years, males at 6–7 years. May live 24 years in captivity, 12 in the wild. Females live longer than males
Voice	Bleating in lambs; short, deep "baa" in adults
Diet	Mainly grasses; also forbs and some shrubs
Habitat	Semiopen rocky terrain; alpine to dry desert
Distribution	Southwestern Canada to western U.S. and northern Mexico
Status	Population: 65,000–68,000; IUCN Least Concern; CITES II. Hunting now controlled, but poaching for horns continues in some areas

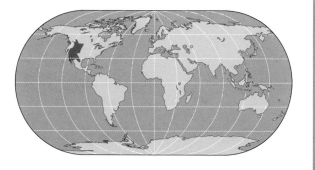

American Bighorn Sheep

Ovis canadensis

American bighorns are stocky sheep that live in the remote deserts and mountains of North America. The rams fight for dominance using their huge horns.

BIGHORN SHEEP ARE PERFECTLY built for life in extreme habitats. They live in remote, rocky places with low vegetation and few trees. There are seven geographical races (sometimes regarded as subspecies). Desert bighorns live in the dry lowland deserts of the southwestern United States and Mexico. Others live in the mountain ranges that stretch from Canada down the western side of North America.

Suited to Harsh Habitats

Bighorns have excellent eyesight and are amazingly agile considering their relative bulk. They can leap up steep, rocky slopes and walk along ledges only a couple of inches wide. Their hooves are well adapted for scrambling over rocky terrain. Their toes are independently movable, separating to grasp either side of stones. The back half of each foot has a round, rubbery pad for extra grip. Most of the plants in the animal's harsh habitats are tough, so the sheep have long, broad molar teeth for grinding and a long rumen for digesting the food as efficiently as possible. The coat has a thick fleecy underlayer. It is brown with a pale rump patch that extends down the back of the legs. The muzzle is also pale. The contrasting markings may help emphasize particular postures so that the sheep are better able to interpret the mood of others in the group.

Rams have massive horns that grow in a tight, sweeping spiral. A ram's horns are used as weapons and shields in fights, and to impress females and rival males. Females also have horns, which are shorter and straighter than those of the male. The horns start to grow when lambs are about two months old and

In fully grown males the horns can be up to 18 inches (46 cm) across and weigh as much as 13 percent of the animal's total body weight.

continue to grow for the rest of their lives, getting wider at the base, as well as longer. Displaying a set of huge horns is a sign that a ram is fit and capable of finding plenty of high-quality food—traits that a female would do well to pass on to her young.

Horns grow faster in summer than in winter, creating annual rings that can be used to assess age, at least for younger animals. Length is a less reliable age guide, since the tips are often worn down from fighting, accidents, and digging. Animals of both sexes use their horns to help clear snow from feeding areas and for grubbing up plants.

Bighorns are sociable animals, living in small groups called bands. Sometimes bands come together to form herds. Most of the time males and females live in separate bands, only linking up in the mating season. Female bands are usually five to 15 animals. Their numbers increase during the spring lambing season. Males live in bands of two to 12, with an average of five animals.

Bighorns are not territorial, but occupy home ranges whose location and size depend on group size, habitat quality, and season. They forage within the home range, wandering steadily but not always following regular trails. They normally walk about 0.2 to 0.5 miles (0.4 to 0.8 km) daily and can travel up to 2 miles (3.2 km) in a day.

Avoiding the Snow

Most populations are migratory to some extent. Some groups merely travel a mile or so up and down the mountainsides, heading to lower ground in the fall as bad weather closes in and snow covers the feeding grounds. In the spring they follow the retreating snow and fresh vegetation to higher ground. Other groups can travel over 35 miles (56 km) in a season, depending on the weather and the quality of food available. Lambs learn the long-distance routes as they follow their mothers.

Bighorns are active during the day, feeding in bouts of one or two hours before resting and chewing the cud. Daytime rest spots are usually in shallow scrapes near the feeding areas. The animals tend to feed close to "escape grounds," areas with rocky precipices and narrow ledges where few predators can follow. At night the sheep retreat to permanent bedding areas on higher ground or to caves where available—again choosing relatively inaccessible places.

The mating season occurs once a year and is called the rut. In northern regions the period is in early winter, from November to December. In the southern desert the rut can last nine

49

months, peaking in August and September. Rams, especially the young ones, are always on the lookout for opportunities for sex. They will attempt to mount females even if they are not in estrus. If there are no females around, males will often mount each other.

Males can tell when a female is in estrus by sniffing her rear and tasting her urine. When a female is in estrus, she becomes more aggressive and determined as she searches for the male with the largest horns. Mating is usually preceded by a chase. It can be a playful, token affair or long and drawn-out, with both animals pausing to rest periodically.

Mating and Habitat

Mating patterns depend partly on the type of habitat the animals live in. On steep, rocky areas with narrow ledges males tend to stick to one female, since visibility is limited, and there is not much room for maneuvering. On more open ground a male can keep an eye on several females and will maintain a harem by chasing away other males. But a female does not always remain with one male and will search for another if "her" male is exhausted from keeping together his harem.

After a gestation period of about 175 days a single lamb is born; twins are rare. In northern parts of their range births of bighorn sheep peak in late April to late June. Before giving birth, the females move to high ground where precipitous slopes provide protection from most predators. A lamb can walk almost immediately after birth and within a day or two is as nimble footed as its mother. Within a couple of weeks a lamb will nibble at grass as well as drinking its mother's milk. Lambs are usually fully weaned by four or five months. Young males tend to leave their mother's band within one to four years. They spend some time wandering alone before

joining a band of rams. Females usually stay with their mother's band for much longer and possibly for life. They reach sexual maturity at four or five years. Rams take longer to reach their adult size, normally six to seven years.

Mortality is high in the first two years of life. Predators such as wolves, coyotes, and pumas are a serious threat. Golden eagles take a few young lambs, but are not a major predator. Other causes of death include accidents such as falls and avalanches. Such life-threatening incidents can happen to an animal of any age, but weak individuals and inexperienced young suffer most. Parasites and diseases, such as mange, lungworm, and pneumonia, also take their toll.

If the youngsters survive their first couple of years, they stand a fairly good chance of reaching "old age." The average life span is nine years, but females can reach over 20. Males tend to die earlier than females, partly due to the stresses of fighting during the rut.

Bighorns are suffering from many pressures associated with humans. Although they tend to live in remote places, disturbance from tourists can be harmful. A more serious problem is competition for grazing, both from domestic stock and feral horses, donkeys, and other grazers. Competition for resources is a particular problem in winter, when the animals tend to congregate on lower and flatter feeding areas. It is less of a dilemma in summer when the grass grows more vigorously. In the summer months the sheep can also

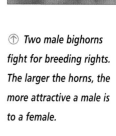

⬆ Two male bighorns fight for breeding rights. The larger the horns, the more attractive a male is to a female.

⬅ A mother suckles her young on the precipitous slopes of the Rocky Mountains. The terrain provides protection from most predators.

retreat to higher and rockier places that are less frequented by other species.

Present Danger

Bighorns have been hunted for many centuries. However, although hunting has been banned or controlled since the early 1900s, the animals are still poached in some areas. The dominant males are especially vulnerable, since their large horns make impressive trophies. Populations have taken a long time to recover from overhunting, partly because females have only one offspring per year.

Battle of the Horns

Males show off their horns in spectacular displays of strength. Such exhibitions are usually enough to signal status and chase off a lower-ranking individual. However, if two rivals are well matched, they will fight for dominance. They stand face to face, then run toward each other. Just before they meet, they rise on their hind legs and throw their full body weight into a crashing head butt. Their skulls are structured to absorb such huge forces, but even so, fights sometimes cause serious injuries and even death.

Common name
Muskox

Scientific name
Ovibos moschatus

Family   Bovidae

Order   Artiodactyla

Size   Length head/body: male 7–9 ft (2.1–2.7 m); female 6–8 ft (1.9–2.4 m); tail length: 3–5 in (7–12 cm); height at shoulder: 47–59 in (120–150 cm)

Weight Male 410–900 lb (186–408 kg); female 353–420 lb (160–190 kg)

Key features Stocky ox with short legs and neck; slight hump at shoulders; large, rounded hooves; coat black with light saddle and front; fur dense and long; sharp, curved horns in both sexes

Habits   Normally active by day; also after dark on long winter nights; social: often forms herds

Breeding   Single calf (twins rare) born late April–mid-June every 2 years after gestation period of 8–9 months. Weaned at 9–12 months; females sexually mature at 2 years, males at 5 years. May live at least 24 years in the wild, probably similar in captivity, but rarey kept

Voice   Bulls roar, calves bleat

Diet   Grasses, lichens, sedges, herbs, and shrubs such as willow and dwarf birch

Habitat   Arctic tundra near glaciers

Distribution Greenland, northern Canada; reintroduced to Alaska, introduced to Russia, Norway, and Sweden

Status   Population: probably around 90,000. Now recovering after populations severely reduced by hunting in 19th century

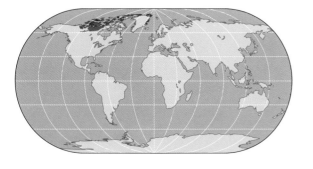

Muskox

Ovibos moschatus

Muskoxen eke out a living in the extremely cold environment of the arctic tundra. Their dense, soft fur keeps them warm. Herds bunch together and face potential predators with a barrier of horns.

MUSKOXEN ARE STOCKY ANIMALS. The thick, shaggy coat and shoulder hump give an illusion of great size, but they are much shorter than an average adult human. Both males and females have horns, but in males the base of the horns (the boss) spreads across the whole forehead. In females it is smaller and divided by a central line of hair. The scientific name *Ovibos* (literally "sheep-ox") refers to the characteristics that the animals share with sheep and cattle. The common name comes from the smell of urine sprayed on their abdominal fur.

Scraping a Living

Muskoxen manage to survive in the arctic tundra—one of the coldest, least productive parts of the world. Here brief, cool summers alternate with freezing winters that last for eight to 10 months of the year. Much of the tundra habitat is bare, rocky ground, and the little vegetation that does exist is low and scrubby. Only the toughest grasses, sedges, and bushes survive the harsh conditions. Plants grow only slowly in such an environment, limiting the numbers of larger herbivores like the muskox that can live here. The oxen often have to scrape away deep or encrusted snow with their front feet to expose the meager plants. In the brief summer grassy river valleys support a few herbs such as alpine lettuce.

Muskoxen do not hibernate as other animals would do in such harsh conditions. Instead, they conserve energy by moving slowly and deliberately across the inhospitable terrain. Daily travel to find food is kept to a minimum, usually between 1 and 6 miles (1.6 and 10 km). Even seasonal migrations are relatively short, generally less than about 30 miles (50 km).

Body design also helps the muskox retain as much heat as possible. The stocky build minimizes heat loss and the long, shaggy coat almost reaches the ground in winter. The guard hairs, which are sometimes over 24 inches (60 cm) long, cover a dense undercoat of soft, light hair. Muskox wool is among the finest found in any large mammal. The fur covers the ears, tail, and scrotum and udder, so that no extremities are left exposed. Muskoxen also bunch together in snow storms and high winds for warmth. Although they are well adapted to the cold, starvation during severe winters—in which snow or ice covers all vegetation—is a major cause of death among the animals.

Muskoxen are basically social animals. Some adult males are solitary during the summer, but most live in bull groups of two to five animals. Females and their young live in mixed-sex summer herds of about 10 individuals. In winter larger herds of up to 50 animals are formed as males join the females, and the small herds aggregate. The rutting season is from August to September, with dominant males keeping other males away from their harems using displays, loud roars, and scent marking.

Clash of the Titans

Clashes between competing males are spectacular. Facing each other, they back away, swinging their heavily horned heads from side to side. When they are far enough apart, they charge at up to 30 miles per hour (50 km/h), meeting with a head-to-head clash of huge force. The broad base of horn at the crown of the head acts as a crash helmet, providing some protection from serious injury. The clashes may be repeated for nearly an hour until one of the pair eventually backs down.

When approached by a wolf, brown bear, or other threat, muskoxen will cluster in a circle or crescent. Young animals are protected in the center, and the enemy is faced by a wall of large feet, heavy heads, and sharp horns. Their behavior works against most predators. However, muskoxen were hunted to near extinction at the end of the 19th century by a combination of settlers, professional hunters, and native peoples using more widely available firearms. Native animals in Canada and Greenland are now protected, and populations were reintroduced to Alaska. Small numbers have also been established on the high ground between Sweden and Norway.

⊕ *A pair of muskoxen on Devon Island, Northwest Territories, Canada. Much of the muskoxen's habitat is bare rocky ground that supports little vegetation.*

Common name Ibex

Scientific name *Capra ibex*

Family Bovidae

Order Artiodactyla

Size Length
head/body: male
47–67 in
(120–170 cm);
female 39–51 in
(100–130 cm); tail length: 5–6 in (12–15 cm);
height at shoulder: 25.5–41 in (65–105 cm)

Weight Male 176–220 lb (80–100 kg);
female 66–110 lb (30–50 kg)

Key features Coat brownish-gray in alpine ibex, various
colors in other subspecies; both sexes have
woolly beard on chin; horns massive and
thick in male, smaller in female, smooth at
back, strong, transverse ridges at front

Habits Mainly active during day; females and young
live in groups; males roam in groups or alone

Breeding Single young (occasionally twins) born late
April–early May after gestation period of
147–161 days. Weaned at 6–7 months;
females sexually mature at 2–4 years, males
at 5–6 years. May live at least 22 years in
captivity, 18 in the wild

Voice Short, whistling hiss

Diet Grasses, herbaceous plants, shrubs, and
lichens

Habitat Rocky alpine crags and deserts

Distribution (Including closely related species described
here) Central Europe; Afghanistan and
Kashmir to Mongolia and central China;
northern Ethiopia, Sudan, Egypt, Syria, and
Arabia; introduced to Slovenia, Bulgaria, and
U.S.

Status Population: (*C. ibex*) about 30,000; IUCN
Least Concern

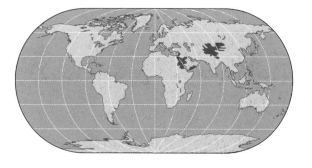

Ibex

Capra ibex

*Ibexes are stocky, sure-footed goats that live high
in the mountains of Europe, Asia, and northeastern
Africa. There are many closely related species, some
of which are threatened with extinction.*

THE QUESTION OF EXACTLY WHAT an ibex is proves to
be a surprisingly complex issue. A type of goat,
it is classified as a member of the goat genus
Capra. Some ibexes now form isolated
populations on mountain tops and in remote
desert areas, where they have been separated
from each other for many thousands of
generations in distinct races.

True Species or Subspecies?

Living apart, there has been ample opportunity
for each form to evolve differently, so much so
that many types of ibex have been described as
separate species. Nevertheless, all forms are
similar genetically. As a result, they are
sometimes treated as a single species divided
into several geographically separate subspecies.
The "true" ibex is the alpine ibex (*Capra ibex*),
which lives in the Alps of western Europe.
Closely related species occur in different parts
of Europe, Asia, and North Africa. They differ
mainly in the size and shape of their horns, and
to a varying degree in their coat color, body
size, and habits. They include the Nubian ibex
of northeastern Africa (*C. nubiana*) listed as
Vulnerable; walia ibex of Ethiopia (*C. walie*),
which is Endangered; Siberian ibex (*C. sibirica*);
west Caucasian tur (*C. caucasica*), which is
Endangered; and east Caucasian tur (*C.
cylindricornis*), which is Near Threatened.

The Nubian ibex is the only ibex that lives in
deserts. It inhabits parts of Arabia and
northeastern Africa. It is smaller than other
ibexes, with a pale, sandy coat that is thought
to reflect some of the intense heat of the
desert. The walia ibex is only found in northern
Ethiopia, where it is now restricted to the
precipitous slopes and crags of the Simien

Ibex horns sweep back in a wide arc and are heavily ridged. In the male they can reach 39 inches (100 cm) in length.

Mountains. It is sleeker than the alpine ibex, with a reddish-brown coat and a black stripe on the front of each leg. The west Caucasian tur has a sturdier body than the alpine ibex, with a thick, strong neck to support the massive horns. It lives in a tiny area in the western Caucasus. The east Caucasian tur is similar to its western neighbor. However, its horns are even bigger and have a gentle spiral shape. The Siberian ibex lives in the high mountains of Central Asia and has horns up to 4.6 feet (1.4 m) long, which may loop back on themselves.

High on the Hills

Ibexes mostly inhabit high, rugged mountainous terrain at 6,500 to 15,000 feet (2,000 to 4,500 m) above sea level. They are sure-footed climbers, jumping up almost vertical slopes, and confidently negotiating narrow ledges above lethal sheer drops. They have a sturdy build, with short, strong legs. Males are larger than females. Both sexes have horns with knobby ridges on the front surface. Those of the male are larger.

Ibexes generally live at or above the tree line and avoid entering dense forests. During winter they move downhill as snow covers their feeding grounds and back up as the snow recedes. However, they feed at the lowest levels during spring to catch the first flush of new grass.

They are most active during early morning and late afternoon, and rest in the shade to avoid the heat of the midday sun. At night they tend to move up to the most precipitous crags in their range to get safely out of reach of predators.

Ibexes spend the summer in small, single-sex herds. The females form maternal herds averaging 10 to 20 animals, while the males are solitary or form bachelor groups. Within the bachelor groups a hierarchy is established based on age, size, and strength. Dominance is tested in clashes during which the males rear up on their hind legs and lock horns with opponents.

In the late fall the males join female herds and stay with them through winter and spring. By now hierarchies have been established, and males tend to avoid each other. High-ranking males claim a harem, which enables the most successful to mate with many females. Kids are born in late spring. They are well coordinated soon after birth and even by their second day can jump. Within a week they are able to follow their mother along all but the most rugged paths. The young join kid groups within the maternal herd.

Distinguishing Features

In the past ibexes were hunted for their horns and also for their body parts, which were thought by some to have medicinal properties. By the early 20th century the ibex was almost extinct. The alpine ibex population dropped to around 60 animals, but with careful protection it now numbers about 3,000 and is no longer threatened. However, other subspecies are still at risk. Uncontrolled hunting is a major threat, particularly in war-torn regions. In some areas ibex have to compete with domestic animals for food and limited space, since people and their agriculture have spread into the mountainsides.

Common name
Mountain goat

Scientific name *Oreamnos americanus*

Family   Bovidae

Order   Artiodactyla

Size   Length head/body: male 4.2–5.2 ft
(1.3–1.6 m); female 45–53 in (115–135 cm);
tail length: 3–8 in (8–20 cm); height at
shoulder: male 35–48 in (90–122 cm); female
31–36 in (80–92 cm)

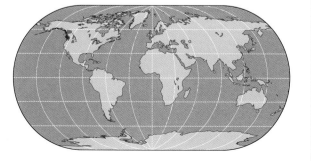

Weight Male 101–309 lb (46–140 kg);
female 101–126 lb (46–57 kg)

Key features Coat yellowish-white with thick, woolly
underfur; long guard hairs form stiff mane on
neck and rump; horns black and curved,
thicker in males; short, strong legs; short tail

Habits   Diurnal, but rests during warmest part of day;
solitary or lives in small groups for most of
year; males fight for dominance

Breeding   Single young or twins born May–June after
gestation period of about 180 days. Weaned
at 3 months; sexually mature at 18 months.
May live about 19 years in captivity, 14 in the
wild (males); females a few more

Voice   Various sheeplike bleating sounds

Diet   Variety of trees, shrubs, grasses, and herbs

Habitat   Steep cliffs, rocks, and edges of glaciers

Distribution Southeastern Alaska and south Yukon to
Oregon, Idaho, and Montana; introduced to
some other mountainous areas of North
America

Status   Population: probably over 100,000. Not
threatened

Mountain Goat

Oreamnos americanus

Mountain goats thrive in cold, craggy terrain, where their white coats make them practically invisible against the snow. Even in summer they look like small patches of snow among the dark rocks, high on the mountainous crags they inhabit.

MOUNTAIN GOATS ARE NOT TRUE goats, but are members of the group known as the Rupicaprini, which literally means "rock goat." Their nearest relatives are the goral (*Nemorhaedus goral*), takin (*Budorcas taxicolor*), and serow (*Capricornis sumatraensis*), which live in Asia, and the European chamois (*Rupicapra rupicapra*). Mountain goats probably reached America via the Bering land bridge when sea levels were lower during the Pleistocene epoch.

Functional Coat

Mountain goats are white or more often a dirty pale yellow, with black, curved horns and short, strong legs. The stockiness is exaggerated by the thickness of their hair, which makes them look squat and thickset. Yet underneath their long coat they are quite slim. The long, stiff guard hairs on the back and shoulders give the goats a pronounced "hump," and thick hair on their upper legs makes them look as if they are wearing short trousers.

However, the long hair is a vital necessity—mountain goats live in some of the coldest, least hospitable places in the United States. They inhabit mountains—usually above the tree line on the edges of major glaciers or snowfields. Their dense coats keep the animals warm in even the most biting wind. The underfur is thick, woolly, and as soft as cashmere. The long guard hairs give some protection against snow and rain, and so prevent the warm underfur from becoming waterlogged. They use their strong front legs to haul themselves up incredibly steep slopes and to brake when coming downhill. Their feet are specially adapted for clambering on loose rock and tiny ledges. A rim of hard, sharp hoof surrounds a flexible rubbery pad, which gives a good grip on even the most slippery rock or ice.

Mountain goats generally have a relaxed life, spending most of their time resting, dust-bathing, and feeding. They eat any plants that are available, browsing on trees and shrubs and nipping the tops off grasses and low herbs. During the summer they spend much of their time on high, rocky ledges, browsing on the small clumps of vegetation that manage to gain a foothold in the crevices or among loose rocks.

⊕ Mothers usually give birth on a high, narrow ledge, well out of reach of predators. Kids are able to walk soon after they are born and quickly learn to negotiate the craggy pathways.

Less often they descend to feed on lush alpine meadows. Females tend to have relatively stable home ranges, while males wander farther. As winter closes in and snow covers their feeding grounds, most mountain goats head for the lower slopes.

Predator Proof

Mountain goats seem unworried by predators. Most potential killers, such as coyotes and lynx, find it difficult to follow the goats up the high, rocky ledges. Small kids are most vulnerable, especially if they become trapped on the lower, less rugged slopes. They are also sometimes taken by golden eagles.

For most of the year males and females do not pay each other much attention. Animals usually feed alone or in small groups of a mother and her offspring. However, interactions can be aggressive when the animals fight for dominance or contest access to limited food supplies. The dominant animal varies, but generally nannies with kids rate highest and gain access to the best food.

Mountain goats do not fight head to head as sheep and true goats do. Instead, they stand side to side, each goat with its head toward the other's rear, tipping their heads to display the sharp-tipped horns. If posturing is not enough to settle disputes, pairs will spin around, trying to jab each other's rump and flanks with their spiky horns. Although the skin on these areas is thick, the short horns are formidable weapons, and animals are sometimes seriously or even fatally injured. Fighting is especially common in the rutting season (November to the end of December). Males scent-mark grass and tree branches by wiping them with oily secretions from glands at the base of their horns.

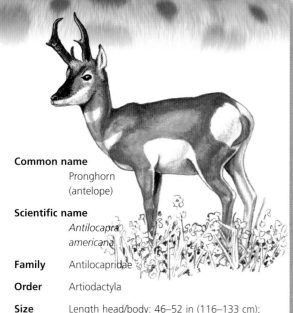

Common name
Pronghorn
(antelope)

Scientific name
*Antilocapra
americana*

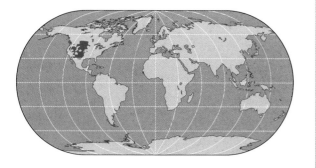

Family Antilocapridae

Order Artiodactyla

Size Length head/body: 46–52 in (116–133 cm);
tail length: 4–5.5 in (10–14 cm); height at
shoulder: about 34 in (87 cm)

 Weight Male 92.5–130 lb (42–59 kg);
female 90–110 lb (41–50 kg)

Key features Long-legged antelope with stocky body;
upperparts pale brown, white belly, flanks,
throat, and rump; males have black face
mask; single forward-pointing prong

Habits Active during day, with short feeding bouts at
night; lives in single-sex herds for most of
year; some populations migratory

Breeding Usually twins born after gestation period of
251 days. Weaned at 4–5 months; females
sexually mature at 15–16 months, males at
2–3 years but breed later. May live 12 years in
captivity, 9–10 in the wild

Voice Grunts and snorts; lambs bleat, males roar

Diet Forbs, shrubs, and grasses; often other plants
such as cacti and crops

Habitat Rolling grassland and bush, especially dry
sage brush country; open conifer forests

Distribution Western U.S., Canada, and some parts of
northern Mexico

Status Population: over 1 million; IUCN Least
Concern; CITES I. Species as a whole no
longer threatened

Pronghorn

Antilocapra americana

*Pronghorns are the only survivors of a once successful
North American antelope family. Their competitive
lifestyle begins even before they are born.*

PRONGHORNS ARE OFTEN REFERRED to as "antelope,"
since they are the only antelope species in the
Americas. They are the fastest runners in North
America, reaching speeds of over 55 miles per
hour (88 km/h) in short sprints. When running
fast, their long legs give them a huge stride of
up to 20 feet (6 m). Their feet end in long,
pointed, cloven hooves that are cushioned for
running on rocks and hard ground.

Avoiding Predators

Speed is an adaptation to help pronghorns live
relatively safely on open habitats, where there
are few places to hide from predators. Being
naturally curious, pronghorns will approach to
inspect signs of movement in the distance, as
do African antelope such as Thomson's gazelles.
However, they are also wary creatures. If
alarmed, they will run away, covering long
distances before stopping to look back. They
have excellent long-distance eyesight, their
large protruding eyes giving them 360-degree
vision. Long, black eyelashes act as sun visors.

 Although similar in appearance and
behavior to African antelope, pronghorns are
only distantly related. Similarities are in fact due
to both types of animals becoming adapted to
similar habitats and lifestyles, a process known
as convergent evolution. The pronghorn is the
sole survivor of a once highly successful family
of antelope species (the Antilocapridae) that
roamed North America until the late Pleistocene
epoch about 50,000 years ago. At that time
they would have had to contend with large, fast
predators, including North American lions,
jaguars, and cheetahs. The necessity to escape
speedily perhaps explains why pronghorns
evolved to be such fast runners—a talent they
have retained, although they need it less now.

The horns of the pronghorn are unique. They have given rise to many arguments over the relationship between the pronghorn antelope and other horned ungulates. In the male the horns are large, about 13 to 16 inches (33 to 41 cm) long. They are backward-curving, and both have a single small, forward-pointing prong. Female horns are much smaller, often only 1.6 inches (4 cm) long, and do not have forward-pointing prongs. They may not be present at all. Each horn has a permanent, unbranched bony core, covered in a keratinous sheath that is shed every year after the rut. By renewing the sheath, the antelope can repair broken or frayed horn tips without discarding the whole thing (as deer do with their antlers).

During the rutting season females and males gather in huge herds. Females usually choose the male that has the territory richest in food. Although calves can walk within a few hours of birth, they do not have the stamina to run for long. To avoid predators such as coyotes, mothers hide their calves in long vegetation, only visiting them for a short period each day to groom and nurse them. At about three to six weeks the calves join a nursery herd with other mothers, calves, and yearlings. Males are sexually mature in their second year and leave their mother's group to join a bachelor herd. However, they rarely breed until they have a territory of their own. Females usually stay within their mother's herd.

Competitive Lifestyle

Life for pronghorns is highly competitive, with social status dictating intergroup and sexual relationships. Competition begins even before the calves are born. Four or more eggs may be fertilized at one time; and although all may implant in the uterus wall, usually only two survive. In the very early stages of their growth the fetuses at the top of the uterus produce long, hanging, tubular spikes that pierce and kill the embryos below. When calves join the nursery group, they jostle for top position, butting and chasing each other for the best feeding and resting sites. Larger calves—those born at the beginning of the season—usually win. The social rank they achieve as juveniles is often maintained for the rest of their lives.

⊕ *Male pronghorns use their horns in head-to-head fights, but only if their ritualized displays do not deter rivals.*

59

List of Species

The following lists all the genera and most species of the families of hoofed mammals covered in this volume:

Order Artiodactyla (Part)

Suborder Ruminantia (Part)

FAMILY ANTILOCAPRIDAE

Antilocapra

A. americana Pronghorn; W. U.S .and Canada, parts of Mexico

FAMILY BOVIDAE
Cattle and Antelope

Subfamily Bovinae
Wild cattle and spiral-horned antelope

Bison

B. Bison American bison (Buffalo); N. America

B. bonasus European bison (wisent); now reestablished in Poland, Caucasus, and Russia

Bos

B. frontalis Gaur (Indian bison, seladang); India, Nepal, Bhutan, Bangladesh, Myanmar, China, Thailand, Indochina, and W. Malaysia

B. grunniens Yak; N. Tibetan Plateau, Xinjiang, and Qinghai in China

B. javanicus Banteng; Myanmar, Thailand, and Indochina; Borneo, Java, and Bali (domesticated); feral in N. Australia

B. sauveli Kouprey (gray ox); Cambodia

B. taurus Common cattle; feral in many places

Bosephalus

B. tragocamelus Nilgai (blue bull or bluebuck); peninsular India

Bubalus

B. arnee (*bubalis*) Wild water buffalo, (Asian buffalo, carabao, arni); domestic and feral in Asia, S. America, Europe, N. Africa, N. Australia; true wild water buffalo in India, Nepal, Bhutan, and Thailand

B. depressicornis Lowland anoa; Sulawesi

B. mindorensis Tamaraw; Mindoro, Philippines

B. quarlesi Mountain anoa; Sulawesi

Pseudoryx

P. nghetinhensis Saloa (Vu Quang ox); Annamite Mountains of W.C. Vietnam and Laos

Syncerus

S. caffer African Buffalo; Africa south of the Sahara

Taurotragus

T. derbianus (*Tragelaphus derbianus*) Giant eland; W. and C. Africa, E. Africa, particularly Sudan

T. oryx (*Tragelaphus oryx*) Common or Cape eland; E., S., and C. Africa

Tetracerus

T. quadricornis Four-horned antelope (chousingha); pensinular India

Tragelaphus

T. angasii Nyala; S.E. Africa

T. buxtoni Mountain nyala; Arusi and Bale Mountains in Ethiopia

T. eurycerus Bongo; E., C., and W. Africa; S. Sudan, Kenya, and the Congo

T. imberbis Lesser kudu; Ethiopia, Uganda, Sudan, Somalia, Kenya, and N. and C. Tanzania

T. scriptus Bushbuck; Africa south of the Sahara except for S.W. and N.W. regions

T. spekeii Sitatunga (marshbuck); Victoria, Congo and Zambezi-Okavango river systems

T. strepsiceros Greater kudu; E., C., and S. Africa

Subfamily cephalophinae
Forest duikers

Cephalophus

C. adersi Ader's duiker; Zanzibar, coastal Kenya, and Tanzania

C. brookei Brooke's duiker; Sierre Leone, Liberia, Ghana, Côte d'Ivoire

C. callipygus Peter's duiker; Cameroon and Gabon east through C. African Republic and Dem. Rep. of Congo

C. dorsalis Bay duiker; Guinea-Bissau east to DRC and south to Angola

C. jentinki Jentink's duiker; Liberia and W. Côte d'Ivoire

C. leucogaster White-bellied duiker; Cameroon south and east into DRC

C. maxwellii (*Philantomba maxwellii*) Maxwell's duiker; Nigeria west to Gambia and Senegal

C. monticola (*Philantomba monticola*) Blue duiker; Nigeria to Gabon east to Kenya and south to S. Africa

C. natalensis Red forest duiker; Somalia south to Zimbabwe and Mozambique

C. niger Black duiker; Guinea east to Nigeria

C. nigrifrons Black-fronted duiker; Cameroon to Angola and east through DRC to Kenya

C. ogilbyi Ogilby's duiker; Sierra Leone east to Cameroon, Gabon

C. rufilatus Red-flanked duiker; Senegal to Cameroon east to Sudan

C. silvicultor Yellow-backed duiker; Guinea-Bissau east to Sudan and Uganda to Angola and Zambia

C. spadix Abbott's duiker; Tanzania

C. weynsi Weyn's duiker; DRC, Uganda, Rwanda and W. Kenya

C. zebra Zebra duiker; Sierre Leone, Liberia, Côte d'Ivoire

Sylvicapra

S. grimmia Common duiker; Sub-Saharan Africa except DRC

Subfamily Reduncinae
Kobus

K. ellipsiprymnus Waterbuck; S. Africa north to Ethiopia and S. Sudan; west to Senegal

K. kob Kob; Gambia east to Sudan and Ethiopia, Uganda

K. leche Lechwe; Botswana, Zambia, S.E. DRC

K. megaceros Nile lechwe (Mrs Gray's lechwe); Sudan, W. Ethiopia

K. vardonii Puku; S. DRC, Botswana, Angola, Zambia, Malawi, Tanzania

Pelea

P. capreolus Gray roebuck (Vaal ribbok or rhebuck); S. Africa

Redunca

R. arundinum Southern reedbuck; Africa north to Tanzania and west to Angola

R. fulvorufula Mountain reedbuck; Cameroon, Ethiopia and E. Africa, S. Africa

R. redunca Bohor reedbuck; Senegal east to Sudan and south to Tanzania

Subfamily Aepycerotinae
Aepyceros

A. melampus Impala; S. Africa to Kenya, Namibia to Mozambique

Subfamily Alcelaphinae
Alcelaphus

A. buselaphus Hartebeest (kongoni); Senegal to Somalia, E. Africa to S. Africa

A. lichtensteinii (may be a subspecies of *A. buselaphus*) Lichtenstein's hartebeest; Tanzania, S.E. DRC, Angola, Zambia, Mozambique, Zimbabwe

Beatragus

B. hunteri Hirola (Hunter's hartebeest); E. Kenya and S. Somalia

Connochaetes

C. gnou Black wildebeest (white-tailed gnu); S. Africa

C. taurinus Blue wildebeest (brindled gnu); norther S. Africa to Kenya

Damaliscus

D. lunatus Topi (tsessebe, sassaby, tiangs damalisc, korrigum, bastard hartebeest); Senegal to W. Sudan, E. Africa through to S. Africa

D. pygargus Bontebok (blesbok); S. Africa

D. superstes Bangweulu Tsessebe; N.E. Zambia

Subfamily Hippotraginae
Grazing antelope

Addax

A. nasomaculatus Addax; formerly entire Sahara. Today remnant populations in Mauritania, Mali, Niger, Chad, S. Algeria, W. Sudan

Hippotragus

H. equinus Roan antelope (horse antelope); Gambia to the Somali arid zone, C. Africa to S. Africa

H. niger Sable antelope; C. Africa to Kenya to S. Africa, Angola to Mozambique

Oryx

O. beisa Beisa (fringe-eared oryx); Djibouti, Ethiopia, Kenya, Somalia, Sudan, and Tanzania

O. dammah Scimitar oryx (white oryx); formerly over most of N. Africa, now regarded as Extinct in the Wild

O. gazella Gemsbok (oryx or beisa oryx); Namibia, Angola, Botswana, Zimbabwe, S. Africa and Tanzania north to the Ethiopian coast

O. leucoryx Arabian oryx (white oryx); formerly Arabian Peninsula, Sinai Peninsula; reintroduced into Oman

Subfamily Antilopinae
Gazelles and dwarf antelope

Ammodorcas

A. clarkei Dibatag; Horn of Africa

Antidorcas

A. marsupialis Springbok; southern Africa west of Drakensberg Mountains and north to Angola

Antilope

A. cervicapra Blackbuck; Indian subcontinent

Dorcatragus

D. megalotis Beira; Somalia and Ethiopia bordering the Red Sea and the Gulf of Aden

Eudorcas

E. rufifrons Red-fronted gazelle; from Senegal in a narrow band running east to Sudan

E. thomsonii Thomson's gazelle; Tanzania and Kenya, and an isolated population in S. Sudan

Gazella

G. benettii Indian gazelle; W. and C. India, Pakistan, S.W. Afghanistan, N.and C. Iran

G. cuvieri Edmi; Morocco, N. Algeria, Tunisia

G. dama (*Nanger dama*) Dama gazelle; Sahara from Mauritania to Sudan

G. dorcas Dorcas gazelle (jebeer); from Senegal to Morocco and west through N. Africa and Iran to India

G. gazella Mountain gazelle; Arabian peninsula, Palestine

G. granti (*Nanger granti*) Grant's gazelle; Tanzania, Kenya, and parts of Ethiopia, Somalia, and Sudan

G. leptoceros Slender-horned gazelle; Egypt east into Algeria

G. soemmerringii (*Nanger soemmerringii*) Soemmerring's gazelle; Horn of Africa north to Sudan

G. spekei Speke's gazelle; Horn of Africa

G. subgutturosa Goitered gazelle; from Palestine and Arabia east through Iran and Turkestan to E. China

Glossary

Litocranius
L. walleri Gerenuk; Horn of Africa south to Tanzania

Madoqua
M. guentheri Guenther's dik-dik; N. Uganda east through Kenya and Ethiopia to the Ogaden and Somalia
M. kirkii Kirk's dik-dik; Namibia and S.W. Angola
M. piacentinii Piacentini's dik-dik (silver dik-dik); E. Somalia
M. saltiana Salt's dik-dik; Horn of Africa

Neotragus
N. batesi Pygmy antelope; S.E. Nigeria, Cameroon, Gabon, Congo, W. Uganda, DRC
N. moschatus Sui; from C. South Africa through Mozambique and Tanzania to Kenya
N. pygmaeus Royal antelope; Sierra Leone, Liberia, Côte d'Ivoire, Ghana

Oreotragus
O. oreotragus Klipspringer; Cape to Angola and up E. Africa to Ethiopia; also isolated groups in Nigeria and C. African Republic

Ourebia
O. ourebi Oribi; E. southern Africa, Zambia, Angola, DRC, Tanzania to Ethiopia and west to Senegal

Procapra
P. gutturosa Mongolian gazelle; most of Mongolia and inner Mongolia
P. picticaudata Tibetan gazelle; most of Tibet
P. przewalskii Przewalski's gazelle; China

Raphicerus
R. campetris Steenbok; from Angola, Zambia, and Mozambique south to Cape and in Kenya and Tanzania
R. melanotis Cape grysbuck; S. Cape
R. sharpei Sharpe's grysbuck; Tanzania, Zambia, Mozambique, Zimbabwe

Saiga
S. tatarica Saiga; N. Caucasus, Kazakhstan, S.W. Mongolia, Zinjiang in China

Subfamily Caprinae
Ammotragus
A. lervia Babary sheep (aouydad); N. Africa

Budorcas
B. taxicolor Takin (golden-fleeced cow); W. China, Bhutan, Myanmar

Capra
C. aegagrus Wild goat (bezoar); Greek Islands, Turkey, Iran, S.W. Afghanistan, Oman, Caucasus, Turkmenia, Pakistan, India
C. caucasica West Caucasian tur; W. Caucasus
C. cylindricornis East Caucasian tur; E. Caucasus
C. falconeri Markhor; Afghanistan, N.

Pakistan, N. India, Kashmir, S. Uzbekistan, Tajikistan
C. ibex Ibex; C. Europe, Afghanistan and Kashmir to Mongolia and C. China; N. Ethiopia to Syria and Arabia
C. nubia Nubian ibex; Red Sea area
C. pyrenaica Spanish goat (Spanish ibex); Pyrenees
C. sibirica Siberian ibex; Afghanistan and east to C. China
C. walie Walia ibex; Ethiopia

Capricornis
C. crispus Japanese serow; Japan
C. milneedwardsii Chinese serow; S. and C. China, Southeast Asia
C. rubidus Red serow; Myanmar
C. sumatraensis Mainland serow; tropical and subtropical E. Asia
C. swinhoei Formosan serow; Taiwan
C. thar Himalayan serow; Himalayas

Hemitragus
H. hylocrius Nilgiri tahr; S. India
H. jayakari Arabian tahr; Oman
H. jemlahicus Himalayan tahr; Himalayas; introduced to New Zealand

Nemorhaedus
N. goral Goral (red or common goral); N. India and Myanmar to S.E. Siberia and S. to Thailand

Oreamnos
O. americanus Mountain goat; S.E. Alaska through to Oregon and Montana

Ovibos
O. moschatus Muskox; Alaska to Greenland

Ovis
O. ammon Argalis; Pamir to Outer Mongolia and throughout Tibetan plateau
O. aries Domestic (Soay) sheep; Orkney Islands and St. Kilda, Scotland
O. canadensis American bighorn sheep (mountain sheep); S.W. Canada, W. U.S. and N. Mexico
O. dalli Thinhorn sheep; Alaska to N. British Columbia
O. musimon Mouflon; Asia Minor, Iran, Sardinia, Corsica, Cyprus; widely introduced into Europe
O. nivicola Snow sheep (Siberian bighorn); N.E. Siberia

Panthalops
P. hodgsoni Chiru (Tibetan antelope); Tibet, E. China, N. India

Pseudois
P. nayaur Blue sheep (bhara); Himalayas, Tibet, E. China

Rupicapra
R. pyrenaica Pyrenean chamois; N.W. Spain (Cantabrian Mountains); Pyrenees, C. Apennines
R. rupicapra Chamois; European Alps, Caucasus, Carpathian, and Tatra Mountains, N.E. Turkey, Balkans; introduced to New Zealand

Words in SMALL CAPITALS refer to other entries in the glossary.

Adaptation features of animal that adjust it to its environment; may be produced by evolution—e.g., camouflage coloration
Adult a fully grown animal that has reached breeding age
Amphibian any cold-blooded VERTEBRATE of the class Amphibia, typically living on land but breeding in the water; e.g., frogs, toads, and newts
Anal gland (anal sac) a gland opening by a short duct either just inside anus or on either side of it
Antler branched prongs on the head of male deer, made of solid bone
Aquatic living in water
Arthropod animals with a jointed outer skeleton, e.g., crabs and insects

Biodiversity a variety of SPECIES and the variation within them
Biomass the total weight of living material
Biped any animal that walks on two legs. See QUADRUPED
Boar male pig
Breeding season the entire cycle of reproductive activity from courtship, pair formation (and often establishment of TERRITORY), through nesting to independence of young
Browsing feeding on leaves of trees and shrubs

Cache hidden supply of food; also (verb) to hide food for future use
Canine (tooth) a sharp stabbing tooth usually longer than the rest
Cannon bone a bone formed by fusion of METATARSAL bones in the feet of some FAMILIES
Canopy continuous (closed) or broken (open) layer in forests produced by the intermingling of branches of trees
Carnivore meat-eating animal
Carrion dead animal matter used as a food source by scavengers

Cecum a blind sac in the digestive tract opening out from the junction between the small and large intestines. In herbivorous mammals it is often very large; it is the site of bacterial action on CELLULOSE. The end of the cecum is the appendix; in SPECIES with a reduced cecum the appendix may retain an antibacterial function
Cellulose the material that forms the cell walls of plants
Cementum hard material that coats the roots of mammalian teeth. In some SPECIES cementum is laid down in annual layers that, under a microscope, can be counted to estimate the age of individuals
Cheek pouch a pouch used or the temporary storage of food
Cheek teeth teeth lying behind the CANINES in mammals, consisting of PREMOLARS and MOLARS
Chromosomes strings of genetic material (DNA) within the cell nucleus; responsible for transmitting features from one generation to the next and for controlling cell growth and function
CITES Convention on International Trade in Endangered Species. An agreement between nations that restricts international trade to permitted levels through licensing and administrative controls.
Cloven hoof foot that is formed from two toes, each within a horny covering
Congenital condition an animal is born with
Coniferous forest evergreen forests found in northern regions and mountainous areas dominated by pines, spruces, and cedars
Cursorial adapted for running

Deciduous forest dominated by trees that lose their leaves in winter (or the dry season)
Deforestation the process of cutting down and removing

trees for timber or to create open space for activities such as farming

Delayed implantation when the development of a fertilized egg is suspended for a variable period before it implants into the wall of the UTERUS and completes normal pregnancy. Births are thus delayed until a favorable time of year

Den a shelter, natural or constructed, used for sleeping, giving birth, and raising young; act (verb) or retiring to a den to give birth and raise young or for winter shelter

Dentition an animal's set of teeth

Desert area of low rainfall dominated by specially adapted plants such as cacti

Dewclaw remains of reduced toes at back of an UNGULATE's leg

Diastema a space between the teeth, usually the INCISORS and CHEEK TEETH. It is typical of rodents and lagomorphs, although also found in UNGULATES

Digit a finger or toe

Digitigrade method of walking on the toes without the heel touching the ground. See PLANTIGRADE

Dispersal the scattering of young animals going to live away from where they were born and brought up

Display any relatively conspicuous pattern of behavior that conveys specific information to others, usually to members of the same SPECIES; can involve visual or vocal elements, as in threat, courtship, or greeting displays

Diurnal active during the day

DNA (deoxyribonucleic acid) the substance that makes up the main part of the chromosomes of all living things; contains the genetic code that is handed down from each generation

Domestication process of taming and breeding animals to provide help and useful products for humans

Dorsal relating to the back or spinal part of the body; usually the upper surface

Droppings see FECES and SCATS

Ecosystem a whole system in which plants, animals, and their environment interact

Endemic found only in one small geographical area and nowhere else

Estrus the period when eggs are released from the female's ovaries, and she becomes available for successful mating. Estrous females are often referred to as "in heat" or as "RECEPTIVE" to males

Eutherian mammals that give birth to babies, not eggs, and rear them without using a pouch on the mother's belly

Excrement FECES

Extinction process of dying out in which every last individual dies, and SPECIES is lost forever

Family technical term for a group of closely related SPECIES that often also look quite similar. Zoological family names always end in "idae." Also used as the word for a social group within a species consisting of parents and their offspring

Feces remains of digested food expelled from the body as pellets. Often accompanied by SCENT secretions

Feral domestic animals that have gone wild and live independently of people

Fur mass of hairs forming a continuous coat characteristic of mammals

Fused joined together

Gape wide-open mouth

Gene the basic unit of heredity enabling one generation to pass on characteristics to its offspring

Generalist an animal that is capable of a wide range of activities, not specialized

Genus a group of closely related SPECIES. The plural is genera

Gestation the period of pregnancy in mammals between fertilization of the egg and birth of the baby

Grazing feeding on grass

Gregarious living together in loose groups or herds

Herbivore an animal that eats plants (grazers and browsers are thus herbivores)

Heterodont DENTITION specialized into CANINES, INCISORS, and PREMOLARS, each type of tooth having a different function. See HOMODONT

Homeothermy maintenance of a high and constant body temperature by means of internal processes; also called "warm-blooded"

Home range the area that an animal uses in the course of its normal periods of activity. See TERRITORY

Horns a pair of sharp, unbranched prongs projecting from the head of CLOVEN-HOOFED animals. Horns have a bony core with a tough outer covering made of KERATIN like our fingernails

Hybrid offspring of two closely related SPECIES that can interbreed, but the hybrid is sterile and cannot produce offspring of its own

Inbreeding breeding among closely related animals (e.g., cousins) leading to weakened genetic composition and reduced survival rates

Incisor (teeth) simple pointed teeth at the front of the jaws used for nipping and snipping

Indigenous living naturally in a region; NATIVE (i.e., not an introduced species)

Insectivore animals that feed on insects and similar small prey. Also used as a group name for animals such as hedgehogs, shrews, and moles

Interbreeding breeding between animals of different SPECIES or varieties within a single FAMILY or strain; interbreeding can cause dilution of the gene pool

Interspecific between SPECIES

Intraspecific between individuals of the same SPECIES

Invertebrates animals that have no backbone (or other true bones) inside their body, e.g., mollusks, insects, jellyfish, and crabs

IUCN International Union for the Conservation of Nature, responsible for assigning animals

IUCN CATEGORIES

EX Extinct, when there is no reasonable doubt that the last individual of a species has died.

EW Extinct in the Wild, when a species is known only to survive in captivity or as a naturalized population well outside the past range.

CR Critically Endangered, when a species is facing an extremely high risk of extinction in the wild in the immediate future.

EN Endangered, when a species faces a very high risk of extinction in the wild in the near future.

VU Vulnerable, when a species faces a high risk of extinction in the wild in the medium-term future.

NT Near Threatened, when it is not CR, EN or VU, but is close to qualifying for those categories

LC Least Concern, when a species has been evaluated and does not satisfy the criteria for CR, EN, VU, or NT.

DD Data Deficient, when there is not enough information about a species to assess the risk of extinction.

NE Not Evaluated, species that have not been assessed by the IUCN criteria.

and plants to internationally agreed categories of rarity. See table opposite

Juvenile a young animal that has not yet reached breeding age

Keratin tough, fibrous material that forms hairs, feathers, and protective plates on the skin of VERTEBRATE animals

Lactation process of producing milk in MAMMARY GLANDS for offspring
Leptospirosis disease caused by leptospiral bacteria in kidneys and transmitted via urine

Mammary glands characteristic of mammals, glands for production of milk
Matriarch senior female member of a social group
Metabolic rate rate at which chemical activities occur within animals, including the exchange of gasses in respiration and the liberation of energy from food
Metabolism the chemical activities within animals that turn food into energy
Metatarsal one of the small bones in the ankle or foot, elongated in species that are adapted for rapid locomotion
Migration movement from one place to another and back again, usually seasonal
Molars large crushing teeth at the back of the mouth
Molt process in which mammals shed hair, usually seasonal
Monogamous animals that have only one mate at a time
Montane in a mountain environment
Musk mammalian SCENT
Mutation random changes in genetic material

Native belonging to that area or country, not introduced by human assistance
Natural selection when animals and plants are challenged by natural processes to ensure survival of the fittest
New World the Americas; OLD

WORLD refers to the non-American continents
Niche part of a habitat occupied by an ORGANISM, defined in terms of all aspects of its lifestyle
Nocturnal active at night
Nomadic animals that have no fixed home, but wander continuously

Old World non-American continents. See NEW WORLD
Olfaction sense of smell
Omnivore an animal that eats almost anything, meat or vegetable
Opportunistic taking advantage of every varied opportunity that arises; flexible behavior
Order a subdivision of a class of animals consisting of a series of related animal FAMILIES
Organism any member of the animal or plant kingdom; a body that has life
Ovulation release of egg from the female's ovary prior to its fertilization

Parasite an animal or plant that lives on or within another
Parturition process of giving birth
Pelage furry coat of a mammal
Pelt furry coat; often refers to skin removed from animal as fur
Pheromone SCENT produced by animals to enable others to find and recognize them
Physiology the processes and workings within plants and animal bodies, e.g., digestion
Placenta the structure that links an embryo to its mother during pregnancy, allowing exchange of chemicals between them
Plantigrade walking on the sole with the heels touching the ground. See DIGITIGRADE
Polygamous when animals have more than one mate in a single mating season
Polygynous when a male mates with several females in one BREEDING SEASON
Population a distinct group of animals of the same SPECIES or all the animals of that species
Predator an animal that kills

live prey for food
Premolars teeth found in front of the MOLARS, but behind the CANINES
Promiscuous mating often with many mates, not just one
Protein chemicals made up of amino acids. Essential in the diet of animals

Quadruped an animal that walks on all fours (a BIPED walks on two legs)

Range the total geographical area over which a SPECIES is distributed
Receptive when a female is ready to mate (in ESTRUS)
Reproduction the process of breeding, creating new offspring for the next generation
Retina light-sensitive layer at the back of the eye
Riparian living beside rivers and lakes
Rumen complex stomach found in RUMINANTS specifically for digesting plant material
Ruminant animals that eat vegetation and later bring it back from the stomach to chew again ("chewing the cud" or "rumination") to assist its digestion

Savanna tropical grasslands with scattered trees and low rainfall, usually in warm areas
Scent chemicals produced by animals to leave smell messages
Scrub vegetation dominated by shrubs—woody plants usually with more than one stem
Siblings brothers and sisters
Social behavior interactions between individuals within the same SPECIES, e.g., courtship
Species a group of animals that look similar and can breed to produce fertile offspring
Steppe open grassland in parts of the world where the climate is too harsh for trees to grow
Sub-Saharan all parts of Africa lying south of the Sahara Desert
Subspecies a locally distinct group of animals that differ slightly from the normal

appearance of the SPECIES
Symbiosis when two or more SPECIES live together for their mutual benefit
syndactylous fingers or toes that are joined along their length into a single structure

Taxonomy the branch of biology concerned with classifying ORGANISMS into groups according to similarities in their structure, origins, or behavior. The categories, in order of increasing broadness, are: SPECIES, GENUS, FAMILY, ORDER, class, and phylum
Terrestrial living on land
Territory defended space
Thermoregulation the maintenance of a relatively constant body temperature either by adjustments to METABOLISM or by moving between sunshine and shade
Tines prongs on the ANTLERS of deer
Tundra open grassy or shrub-covered lands of the far north
Tusk enlarged canine tooth that projects beyond edge of mouth

Ultrasounds sounds that are too high-pitched for humans to hear
Underfur fine hairs forming a dense, woolly mass close to the skin and underneath the outer coat of stiff hairs in mammals
Ungulate hoofed animals such as pigs, deer, cattle, and horses; mostly HERBIVORES
Urea toxic waste derived from the digestion of proteins
Uterus womb in which embryos of mammals develop

Ventral the belly or underneath of an animal (opposite of DORSAL)
Vertebrate animal with a backbone (e.g., fish, mammals, reptiles), with skeleton made of bones, but sometimes cartilage
Vocalization making of sounds such as barking and croaking

Zoologist person who studies animals
Zoology the study of animals

Useful Websites

General

http://animaldiversity.ummz.umich.edu/
University of Michigan Museum of Zoology animal diversity websites. Search for pictures and information about animals by class, family, and common name. Includes glossary

http://www.cites.org/
IUCN and CITES listings. Search for animals by scientific name, order, family, genus, species, or common name. Location by country; explanation of reasons for listings

http://endangered.fws.gov
Information about threatened animals and plants from the U.S. Fish and Wildlife Service, the organization in charge of 94 million acres (38 million ha) of American wildlife refuges

http://www.iucn.org
Details of species and their status; listings by the International Union for the Conservation of Nature, also lists IUCN publications

http://www.nccnsw.org.au
Website for threatened Australian species

http://www.ewt.org.za
Website for threatened South African wildlife

http://www.panda.org
World Wide Fund for Nature (WWF), newsroom, press releases, government reports, campaigns

http://www.aza.org
American Zoo and Aquarium Association

http://www.wcs.org
Website of the Wildlife Conservation Society

http://www.nwf.org
Website of the National Wildlife Federation

http://www.nmnh.si.edu/msw/
www.nmnh.si.edu/msw/
Mammals list on Smithsonian Museum site

http://www.press.jhu.edu/books/walkers
_mammals_of_the_world/prep.html
Basic text, including illustrated species listing

Specific to this volume

http://www.awf.org
The African Wildlife Foundation website, carries information on giraffes

http://www.ultimateungulate.com
Includes information on all ungulate families

http://www.bds.org.uk
The website of The British Deer Society

Picture Credits

Front Cover: iStockphoto: Four Oaks (tl); Shutterstock: Larsek (tr), Magdalena Bujak (bl), Johan Swanepoel (br)

Disc image: Shutterstock: Paul Banton

Ardea: Yann Arthus-Bertrand 32-33, Ferrero-Labat 20-21, 21, Kenneth W. Fink 24-25, Francois Gohier 56-57; **Corbis:** Ecoscene/Ian Harwood 22-23, Hulton 16, Carl & Ann Purcell 36-37, Lynda Richardson 26-27, Kennan Ward 52-53, Zuckerman 34-35; **FLPA:** Minden Pictures 16-17, Mark Newman 58-59, Jurgen & Christine Sohns 18-19, Terry Whittaker 15; **Nature PL:** Ingo Arndt 54-55, Peter Blackwell 32, Torsten Brehm 40-41,

Jeff Foott 50, 50-51; **Photolibrary Group:** Daniel J. Cox 42-43, Mike Hill 38-39, Stan Osolinski 30-31, 48-49, David Tipling 11b, Tom Ulrich 12-13; **Photoshot:** Daryl Balfour 46-47, Nigel J. Dennis 28-29, T. Kitchen & V. Hurst 14, Stephen Krasemann 11t; **Premaphotos Wildlife:** K. G. Preston-Mafham 44-45.

All Artworks Brown Reference Group